LAYERS OF TRUTH

NAVIGATING THE OBJECTIVE FROM THE SUBJECTIVE

DREW WEATHERHEAD

Copyright © 2024 by Drew Weatherhead

All rights reserved. No part of this publication may be reproduced, stored or transmitted in any form or by any means, electronic, mechanical,

photocopying, recording, scanning, or otherwise without written permission from the publisher. It is illegal to copy this book, post it to a website, or distribute it by any other means without permission.

First edition

CONTENTS

Foreword   5

Prologue   9

CHAPTER I

1. INTRODUCTION   13
   What is true and what is Truth   17
   Stratified Truth   26
   What constitutes a layer?   32
   The Three Pillars of Perception   38

CHAPTER II

2. TRUTH IN SCIENCE   45
   The Empirical Model   48
   The Demon in the Method   50
   The Heist of History   56
   When Science Goes Wrong   60
   A Problem with the Brain   63
   Smoke and Mirrors   69
   Think of the Children   75
   Of Mice & Men   78
   Logic and Rationalism   91
   A Construct of Layers   97

CHAPTER III

3. TRUTH IN PHILOSOPHY   105
   Philosophic Rationality   108
   What Is and What Ought   113
   The Man Who Murdered God   133
   Below The Surface   141

CHAPTER IV

4. TRUTH IN THEOLOGY ... 159
   A Problem of Terms ... 161
   The Linchpin Fence ... 163
   England's Most Reluctant Convert ... 167
   Of Religions And Creeds ... 171
   Blending The Philosophic Towards The Theologic ... 177
   Philosophical Theologies ... 181
   Getting Behind Consciousness ... 184
   The Problem of Suffering ... 192
   Death and the Ethereal ... 198
   A Higher Power ... 201
   Closing of the Circle ... 205
   The Return of God ... 208

CHAPTER V

Conclusion ... 213

Epilogue ... 233

FOREWORD

Truth is a much less straightforward concept than most of us care to admit.

It is not something we can hold in our hands and observe from every angle. It is something we live within and can glimpse only in part... in passing... and only rarely with great clarity.

And this is the value of *Layers of Truth*. Through the following pages we can see laid out before us – simply, concisely, but with great depth – just how limited our understanding of 'truth' really is.

And not just limited in the sense that we cannot grasp it in its entirety... but that we are trained to see truth itself as limited. As something that can fit easily within the scientific framework itself. Something that can be shrunk, reduced, and limited to such a degree that we can know it and grasp it, fully.

But as the reader will see, this is a lie. Or at the very least a minimization of the truth. A reduction of *emmet* (Hebrew meaning: total truth) into fact (a bit of verifiable information).

And this conflation of truth and fact is responsible for so much of the confusion, imbalance, and dis-ease that plagues the human psyche in 2024.

We have stripped everything down to it's factual foundation. To the point of removing beauty and goodness and awe from the human experience entirely... because they are just subjective and thus without value in a world that cares only for the objective.

We have told young men and women that the spirit is largely just a figment of our imagination, and the body is all that is real. We've told these same young people that 'values' (what used to be known as morality) is nothing more than subjective, arbitrary preference. And in doing so we have stripped away from the young everything that resembles...

Hope.

As C S Lewis prophetically wrote:

"We make men without chests and expect from them virtue and enterprise. We laugh at honor and are shocked to find traitors in our midst. In a sort of ghastly simplicity we remove the organ and demand the function. We make men without chests and expect of them virtue and enterprise."

It is, in my view, this fundamental error that Drew so beautifully addresses in *Layers of Truth*. We know the epistemological value of science – but we have forgotten the equally (or perhaps more) valuable epistemology of philosophy and theology. And it is only armed with these three pillars of knowing that any person can truly face the tragedies and triumphs of the human experience.

Drew masterfully weaves together the history and importance of science, philosophy, and theology to show the importance of each – indeed of all – to a genuine and real pursuit of truth. At the same time, he shows just how elusive the very concept of 'truth' is. By the end of these pages the reader will not only have a solid foundation of each of these three concepts but also a humility that so many intellectuals in the 21st century lack: the deep knowledge that truth is, in so many ways, terrifyingly beyond us and nearly inaccessible in its entirety.

But! That we can also approach it, come near to it, and know it to such a degree that our lives become not just more effective but greatly enriched.

In other words, readers might learn that we cannot truly love Truth until we fear it, nor can we properly fear it until we love it.

During the last 12 months Drew and I have had weekly conversations on his podcast, The Social Disorder, and it is a pleasure to see so many of the seeds planted in these conversations taken to such a deeper place – and detailed with admirable precision – in these pages.

To be blunt, this book is a demolition of the casual, dismissive, arrogant assumptions of most modern intellectuals: that any non-scientific approach to truth is immature and wasteful. Instead, Drew replaces this hubris with a beautiful vision of a human experience defined by the interplay of science, philosophy, and theology. He shows that these three pillars support, enhance, and require each other for the human mind to have even a glimpse of emmet, or total truth.

This book is an antidote to the chestless ideologies that plague modern man and I am honored to be able to introduce it to you here.

~ Matt Enns,
Ottawa, ON, Canada
Feb 29, 2024

PROLOGUE

To the reader,

I don't know how you came upon reading this book. If you know me personally, tangentially, or not at all.

I'm not a man of academic repute or intellectual credential. I am an average person drawn by strange fate to write about a titanic topic. If you require of an author notable status or laudable public standing, this book will start quite shy of those standards.

If instead you, like myself, have become enamored by the confusion and paradoxes of what people present as Truth in your time, I hope that these writings can help.

It's strange to me; I find so often that I'm drawn by some intangible force towards a wave that stirs up throughout humanity. In the time that I set out towards the writing of this book, the topic of Truth was an undercurrent. Something that wasn't being spoken directly to by name. But in the proceeding months, as I grew ever closer to completing this work, it became self-evident that *many* other people were themselves also caught up by this same undercurrent. The swell of it was becoming culturally apparent shortly before I wrote my final chapter. This grassroots level, invisible calling had unexpectedly breached the surface of mainstream consciousness.

In the time of my own pondering on this subject, I thought myself alone. Some name less author writing about ideas that were left-field of culture. Little did I realize the timeliness of what took me nearly a year of writing.

Whatever powers of fate, or chance, or divinity called me to write what I wrote when I wrote it, looking back now, it seems so obviously meant for this time.

And so, dear reader, who ever you are and how ever you found this chronicling of my thoughts, may it find you in the time that you needed it for the reasons you needed it most.

~Drew Weatherhead

CHAPTER I

WHAT IS TRUE & WHAT IS TRUTH

"Sometimes a heavy dose of truth, a pure injection of reality, is what we need, the kind of medicine that liberates the soul."

— MATTHEW ARNOLD

INTRODUCTION

> "There are two ways to be fooled. One is to believe what isn't true; the other is to refuse to believe what is true."
>
> — SOREN KIERKEGAARD

The simplest concepts in life have a pattern to them. They start off, at first, appearing obvious. Upon further analysis though, they seem to break into endless pieces that wind up complicating, redefining, and even contradicting the simple idea you began with.

Those of us who make the effort towards these analyses find ourselves in an unexpected conundrum; either we become disenfranchised by the entire notion of the concept or we work diligently to organize the panacea of disparate pieces into a construct of its own.

The former is a path of despair and subjective chaos. The destroying of, perhaps, a foundational concept that your worldview rested firmly upon. That path may lead to the ruination of one's ability to parse the world they thought they knew, leading them deeper and farther into a vortex of nihilism and pain.

The latter is one of creation and hope. Where (in the face of emergent confusion) you discover a nascent opportunity for you to more acutely explore, experiment, and understand that which you unwittingly took for granted.

This book is my personal attempt to both explore and present the many faceted layers of what most people consider a self-explanatory concept.

Something so basic and obvious, a toddler understands it. Yet, as fundamental as it may be, something that, when broken apart, presents diametric dilemmas and circuitous paradigms… Something as basic as Truth.

When I was a child, the world at large was an endless ocean of possibility. I had a powerful imagination and a comparably insatiable curiosity. Every day was a new adventure where I searched to expand my knowledge through every means available.

Often times, that search would consist of my own experiences. But, nearly as often, I would take in information from third-party sources to both expand and bolster my existing level of understanding.

What I didn't realize I was doing in this process, which is now more explicitly clear, was a curating of my own personal perception of the universe. In the efforts I took to expand my own horizons, I simultaneously structured a proprietary construct of my internal reality. Not only by the addition of new information but also by the omission of other information. Whether it was complimentary or contradictory, whatever information I accrued through whatever means I came by it would wind up being my personal version of reality.

This, however normal (in fact, universal), act of individualization is so front loaded into our formative years that a large portion of who we are consciously and subconsciously emerges out of it. But what I, and many other people like me, didn't realize for decades after was that my perception was a construct at all. I, just as many others, presumed that I knew reality due to my explorations of yesteryear to a degree that set me in the position of knowing *Truth*. Any other information I learned beyond that was more or less a more granular resolution of what I already knew.

What I would discover years later, though, was how limited my conception of total reality was in practice and by necessity. In fact, the degree to which everyone, past and present, built and relied upon customized, man-made paradigms to map their realities onto was a revelation that shattered my foundations in a radical way.

In my previous book, *Consciousness Reality & Purpose*, I spent a significant amount of time elucidating how little humanity knows (and can possibly know) of total reality. Even the breadth and height to which total reality may stretch is, in itself, beyond our feeble comprehension. The more we try to understand, the more complex and convoluted our previous understanding becomes. Each question asked fractalizes into answers that beg a thousand more questions.

It was through this realization that our place within reality became more apparent. We simply cannot know all of total reality. What's worse, we cannot know what, among the unquantified amount of total reality we don't know, is vitally connected to that which we do. But knowing that this is (and must always be) the state of human understanding, it becomes clear that everything we think we know — both subjectively and communally — is a conceptualized structure, not an explicit *Truth*.

Take the time it may require to fully absorb the weight of that last statement. Because it could come as an affront to anyone who believes they know the Truth. Especially to anyone who was simply taught what the Truth is without ever questioning or exploring around what they were taught. For if we can't know what we don't know, and what we don't know could wildly amend what we do, who can be concretely sure that the Truths they trust are (at the least) complete or (at the most) real in the end?

You may, at this point, start to feel your guard going up. The conclusions and contradictions arising in your mind may be sounding warning bells and striking defensive stances.

Now, this is the point I mentioned at the outset of this chapter; a fork after which point you must branch towards either a totalizing nihilistic dissolution of the primacy you rested your trusted worldviews upon or an opportunity to expand and more greatly refine a new understanding to replace it in its stead.

WHAT IS TRUE AND WHAT IS TRUTH

The questions that you will likely start to wrestle with after these considerations are sure to be the same as I have in my own experience.

I was raised knowing the Truth. In all things I was sure what I knew was self-evidently true. That makes it the Truth then, right?

But if my understanding of Truth is constrained within my own personal construct of what I've known up until now, even however supplemented by "Truths" I've absorbed by proxy from other people's considerations (which themselves are limited to *their* own understanding), is it even *possible* for anyone to know Truth?

Before we confront that question, and confront it we must, it's incumbent upon me to first take the time to define some critical terms before we continue further.

One of the hidden filters that exists within the experience of being human lies between the point that a thought arises and the subsequent translation of that thought into language. You may think that you think in words. But then why can we stumble for the right words when trying to express a thought? The thought itself is something of a preordination. It precedes the effort our mind makes to attribute it to specific words within a specific dialect of a specific lexicon. This, by nature, creates a de-resolution of the thought itself by the time it can be expressed externally.

With this in mind, and because the purpose of this writing is my attempt at most accurately transmitting the thoughts I have to the reader, I want to define what I mean by the words *true* and *Truth*.

The words themselves, as they're defined by standard English dictionaries, don't define the distinction I'm trying to convey in this book. So, permit me to present the ideas I mean to be represented by these two important terms throughout your reading ahead.

When I invoke the word *true* within the construct I intend to build out, it's meant to convey something being correct or accurate. This is what some people refer to as 'small-t truth'. It's meant as a lower-case imbuing of situational accuracy that is, by nature, constrained within whatever contextual parameters are set by a conversation about a specific thing.

For example, it is true to state that the sky is blue within the parameters of a subjective human description of a clear midday's sky. Though if you were to add another constraining parameter of a dog's subjective view of the same sky, the color blue is no longer a true description. Small 't' truth is reliant upon an exact defining of what is being discussed and specifically within preordained parameters. So, for the purposes of these writings, this is what is meant when I use the word *true*.

In contrast, when I use the word *Truth*, I intend to convey something much more totalizing. More correspondent beyond narrow parameters. In fact, one of the best descriptions of the 'big-T' Truth I intend to use for my purposes is found within the Hebrew word for Truth: אֱמֶת (pronounced Emmet). Emmet is a word that, in the Hebrew language, uses the beginning, middle, and last letters of their alphabet to convey the idea that Truth is the entire Truth — from the beginning through to the end. Total reality. Total Truth.

To keep the distinction between these two terms obvious as we progress through the remainder of this book, I will be capitalizing *Truth* and keeping the word *true* in lowercase. (Something I'm sure the grammatically savvy readers have already picked up on.)

Now that I've defined my terms, let's return to the question I proposed previously. Is it even possible for anyone to know Truth?

If total Truth is analogous to total reality, then we find ourselves yet again constrained within our own limited personal and communal understanding of it. If we do not and likely cannot know all of total reality, how can we propose to know emmet; the total Truth? And in this position, what is the likelihood that what we think is the Truth is only a fragment of the total Truth? And what's more, if what we consider Truth is incomplete, what among the remaining total Truth may either compliment (or even be vital to) the Truth fragment we claim to know?

In 1999, clinical psychologist and professor Jordan Peterson released a book titled *Maps of Meaning*. In this book, one of the prevailing themes that guided its exploration into the way that people and cultures view the world around them was that of chaos and order. Another analogous dichotomy, as Peterson would present, is that of the *known* and the *unknown*. In the category of *order*, one can retain all that is known. Once something is known it can further be categorized into other important distinctions, such as dangerous or safe. Knowing something, even if that knowledge is potentially terrifying, is the preferable state-of-being for any higher functioning, conscious creature. Conversely, the category of *chaos* is everything that remains *unknown*. To encounter something that is unknown presents a state-of-being that is perpetually insecure and rife with anxiety. For if you don't know where a thing rests on a spectrum ranging from totally safe and totally deadly, the chance of it being either is equally possible. That's a state of total chaos and anarchy.

It goes without saying that the benefit of knowing something versus not knowing something is more than important, it could be *existentially* vital. The dilemma that we, as rational and cognizant human beings, run up against is that if we cannot know all things, then there will be a necessary and inevitable amount of our existence that remains in the state of chaos. Psychologically, this is a realization that most people simply cannot abide. It creates a steady state of unease and baseline fear that will weigh on anyone's psychological faculties. Logically leading one further down a path of declining mental health and potential nihilistic despair. What is a person to do under the auspice of such an existence? Most often, we turn to the same process that helped us categorize and relegate the realm of the known to begin with.

Being that the task of discovering and structuring what is known in our lives is one we must each do for ourselves, what that effectively does is make us our own, sole arbiter of Truth. Regardless of whether the *known* we are categorizing was self discovered or acquired from external sources, the job of accepting (and subsequently ordering) it is only ever done by us. The framework that is produced from this process will be, in many ways, proprietary to each individual. As unique as your fingerprint, similar to many, but different from all. We can't even help the differences between each of our own internal lattices of understanding. Even if everyone was only ever taught the very same explicit facts, each person decides which of them they will internalize as true. On top of that, they add the experiences they personally have, which offers another dimension of difference. But the greatest convolution within each of our individualized frameworks of reality is the degree to which they are informed by our subconscious mind. Our internal neural net of all that is known is constantly and radically refined by subconscious stimuli and autonomic rationalization that we don't even consciously know is happening, let alone hold any agency over to prevent. So no matter the person, their intelligence or acuity, our perception of Truth is inextricably constrained within the limited and unique architecture of order that we've built from what we've known.

We define what is true, and as such, define what we consider Truth. Although by so doing, we take on the responsibility of not only testing and knowing what is true (thereby constituting what must be Truth), but also understanding the difference between the two so as not to conflate one with the other.

What so often happens, unbeknownst to many who do it, is the mistaken conflation of something that is true for what is hence considered the Truth. As you will see in later chapters, this tendency leads not just to false Truths being espoused by individuals but also towards the means for malicious or malevolent actors to use this methodical conflation for the purpose of funneling others into a prescribed Truth that may be entirely false!

The human mind is, in a large way, a pattern finder. Once patterns are found, they are categorized somewhere amidst our network of the known. We are *so* good at finding and organizing patterns that we can very easily (knowingly or unknowingly) construct a pattern, adhoc, to suit a psychological or sociological need. Since we are the arbiters of our perception of Truth, we retain the agency to accept or reject information as true. If we *want* something to be true that would help us justify what we consider is Truth, it's not only well within our ability to do so, we are the only oversight within the process. We alone are the judge, jury, and defender of what is true. And we are exquisitely talented at constructing patterns to justify our Truths. You could call it lying but, in essence, what it is is story telling.

Humans, individually and as a whole, rationalize through story. Story is the only way we have to express our thoughts to others or even to qualify information we encounter ourselves. Everything we think, experience, learn, or communicate is some transmutation of a story. Whether from direct, raw data or from someone else's stories being absorbed through your own mind's filter. Renown grandfather of psychology Carl Jung was one of the first modern thinkers to make explicit the fact that people don't parse the world in data, we chunk data based upon its relevance within recognizable icons or archetypes. When you look at a tree you don't first quantify it in size, or colors, or any of its constituent parts; you first see it as a tree. 'Tree' is a known archetype, a broad category among what is known. Whereas the information that pertains to that tree is supplementary to the archetype 'tree'. Even thought itself requires a filter of known icons or archetypes that tell the story of what the thought is before it can be rationalized within your mind, let alone if you hope to present it externally. Words themselves are stories, with detailed etymological histories and culturally constructed intentionality. You could go so far as to say that the letters we use to represent our words are themselves microcosms of the same dynamic.

As it turns out, there is nothing more natural than the process of storytelling to a human. It's vital to every stage of what gives us the ability to parse our reality at all. So we now come back to the question: what is a person to do with the knowledge that everything they know as Truth is subject to their own limited understanding of total reality? With such a potentially infinite and relevant portion of reality that will always remain unknown, we do what comes most naturally to us — we make up stories.

Even a story (whether implicit or explicit) about something that is unknown creates something that can be categorized as *known*. This is the universal fix-all that humanity has used since time immemorial to feel safe and secure in a never ending landscape of chaos. And it's made possible (and even logical) by our ability (and propensity) to manipulate what is true by setting critical parameters via story.

You could then say that everything we accept as true is reliant upon, and relative to, any given story. A story is vitally entwined with something being qualified as true. But the Truth is, in contrast, something more absolute. Truth isn't dependent upon or relative to story, even though we ourselves are constrained in our attempts to express Truth through it.

Therein lies the crux of the matter. The thing that is most crucially important, if we hope to be able to reliably navigate reality, is the Truth. Yet the enormity of it will forever be light-years beyond our ability to know. The total Truth, emmet. Its existence is undeniable, yet its containment is impossible. It's with this unavoidable paradox in mind that I've come to the following conclusion: Something of a structure, or meta-huristic, to help elucidate what we can of the total Truth in a way that helps to categorize and disconnect our limited perspective from that of a linear or binary constraint to that of a more three-dimensional and interconnected galaxy of layers.

STRATIFIED TRUTH

When I began to notice not only the distinction between true and Truth but also the tendency for people to either knowingly or unknowingly conflate the two, I saw the issue from a game theoretic perspective.

On one hand, people were knowingly presenting something as true within their own carefully constructed parameters for the purpose of falsely presenting it as the Truth of a thing. The benefits of this are obvious and ubiquitous. Anyone with the ability to skillfully architect a narrative (a story) wherein the outcome reached a predetermined and beneficial result (something that was true within the scope of the narrative it was constrained), a powerful tool of manipulation becomes available that can be used to construct a false reality to serve their needs.

On the other hand, if a person didn't realize that what they were perceiving as true was only narrowly and conditionally so, the ignorance of not understanding this critical conflation leaves open the possibility for them to be fooled into anything. Certainly by those who understand the difference and how to wield it as a tool. But also by those ignorant people themselves who, being human, are apt to and adept at personal narrative creation to ease their troubled minds by the sorting of terrifying unknowns into their inner category of the known. Even if the inappropriate placement of them by these means, in reality, leaves them open to the actual Truth that may blind-side them, in defiance of their faulty beliefs, at any time in the future.

In the game theoretic sense, the former person is playing a game they understand at a level that allows for them to take advantage of those who don't. While the latter person is haplessly trapped in a game they don't even realize is being played —being endlessly and effortlessly controlled by either those craftier players or their own subconscious — while left wondering why the world seems to conspire against them despite them 'knowing' the Truth.

It's difficult, if not impossible, to be able to navigate such a game if you play the role of the hapless and ignorant. But even those who understand what they're doing by manipulating and malleating stories to produce something true may, for their efforts, be avoiding or even denying what the Truth of the matter is to themselves. This equates to it's own form of illusory reality. Not for the faulty acceptance of something true as the Truth, but by the absence of knowing or even looking for what is the Truth even while knowing that what they're doing is a facade of it.

Just as you can have a lie of omission, you can retain an ignorance of Truth while still understanding what you profess of a thing as being (at best) conditionally true. Though they may know they are playing a game, they still don't know (and sometimes don't care about) the Truth. This leads to a faulty reality for lack of Truth in a similar way that those they fool accept a faulty reality by the admission of a conditionally true lie.

In the observation of this game being played in every arena of the world — from the internal to the interpersonal, the philosophical to the metaphysical, the scientific to the societal — I began to see a trend, or theme, emerge that has since helped me to track when and how the differences between what is true and what is *Truth* divide. The concept is that of layers.

As the physical world can be broken up and subdivided into disparate (yet interconnected) layers of scope, similarly does Truth exist at all layers (no matter the scope) but may not transpose directly one to another. If the total Truth is the beginning, middle, and end, then a fragment of it must exist at all possible layers that it could divide into. This is where I'd like to present, for the sake of my construct, a third unit of consideration: Truth fragments.

A Truth fragment is a piece of total Truth, a constituent part of the whole, that exists in and subsumes a total layer. That is to say, within a layer there is everything that is true regarding it. All of the *small-t* true things, when combined completely, constitute the Truth of that layer. Being that each layer is only a fragment of total Truth, it is not emmet, but is complete within its scope. Therefore, a Truth fragment is all that could be known within any layer in question. You can focus on any number of true things within a given layer, but you require every single true thing about it to constitute a complete Truth fragment of emmet.

In the same way that you can conflate something true as the Truth at any given layer of consideration, a complete Truth fragment can be conflated as true at all levels. This is a mistake. If you know everything there is to know about your foot — all of the true things that complete it as a Truth fragment — the entirety of that knowledge doesn't follow to your hip, or your back. Even though they are connected to the whole, each fragment is complete within itself yet unique in comparison to disparate layers.

That's not to say that what may be true within one layer may not also be true within another (like there being veins or cells in each fragment of your body). But the distinction comes from the level of difference, not similarity, from one layer to the next. Every layer of difference is distinctive due to the totality of its Truth fragment, not simply a similarity of things that are true within it as compared to another layer.

Finally, within a total Truth fragment, there can be another partition of use— subsets. These are a grouping of true things within a single Truth fragment that relate to each other enough to have reliable utility, but don't require the *entirety* of the Truth fragment to do so. Think of subsets as bubbles or bundles of true things within a layer. Those bubbles can be added to with any other true thing that affords greater utility within the same layer, but until every true thing is known of the Truth fragment they reside within, they will always be considered incomplete.

This is the construct I intend to utilize throughout the remainder of this book. To simplify it, starting from the top and moving to the bottom: Total Truth (emmet), Truth fragment (everything that is true within a layer), subset (a grouping of true things within a layer that affords utility), something that is true (a solitary true thing that may exist in many different layers).

Broadly, we will be looking at differing layers of Truth. How they exist within varying layers of reality, like the material, the ethereal, and the cognitive. How they can affect each other, how they can contradict each other, and how they can compliment (even more highly resolve) each other in their relations.

Part of the unavoidable responsibility each person has in their own, unique journey within total reality is the proprietary construction of their perception. This is fully informed not only by way of how much they know, and not even of how much of any given Truth fragment they know; but by the interplay of everything they know within every layer they know things within.

Consider a piano with no keys. In this simplistic example, you may add one key for every Truth fragment you know. It may be that no one could realistically add an entire key, but, for the sake of analogy, let's say that you can. Perhaps, after decades of dedicated effort, you've added five keys. How many songs can you play with them? Theoretically, the number is infinite. In that sense, it may seem that you have access to total Truth. Yet, you are still missing dozens of other keys. Would the addition of those keys change the number of songs you could play on them? No. Infinity is infinite. But the possible complexity through the interconnectivity of so many more harmonious keys lends a more robust and abundant tapestry to your possible perception of the whole.

It's through the addition of keys, the omission of keys, and the way that those two things interact in practice that defines what we consider our reality. Our individual constraints constitute both our uniqueness and the opaqueness of the reality we exist within.

Though, once the concept of layers within emmet has been proposed, certain obvious questions arise to the curious mind. Questions like:

- What constitutes a layer?
- Is there overlap between layers? and
- How do you distinguish layers apart from one another?

These are important considerations if one hopes to construct any sort of comprehensible structure. So I will attempt to further define what layers are and how they can be partitioned and assembled in various ways so as to help the reader identify and organize the keys on their own piano.

WHAT CONSTITUTES A LAYER?

In 1956, American psychologists Paul Meehl and Lee Cronbach produced a hallmark paper titled "Construct Validity in Psychological Tests". Its aim was to define, as clearly as possible, how scientists and philosophers could test their constructs when the subject of them isn't empirical by nature. Subjects like emotional states or societal traits that are difficult to quantify or rationalize within an arbitrary measurement.

Although this particular issue had been one that science had been wrestling with for at least 15 years prior; this paper was seen to aggregate and codify the efforts of everyone who had been concerned about it into something that could be used as some sort of standard of practice.

There have been competing versions of construct validation theories put forth in the decades to follow, but no matter which version is cited or used in practice they all rest upon some version of triangulation from other related or peripheral modes. Simply put, the validity of a construct becomes more likely the more other conceptual frameworks concur or validate it. Similar to the way that you can use geographical triangulation to pin point the accuracy of a position on a map, the more differing 'points' or perspectives of consideration fit the construct in question, the higher its conceptual validity is thought to be.

With this guiding principle in place, the following conceptual definition is what I propose to constitute a layer of Truth.

1. A layer can be intuitively distinct without significant explanation.
2. A layer involves many true things within it. The fewer the 'small-t' true things make it up, the lower the likelihood it is a layer.
3. Distinguishable layers of Truth can be found peripherally around any given layer.
4. An action applied to proposed layers that are considered related, or proximal in concept, produces differing results.
5. Adjusting the scope or scale of a known layer reveals different layers based upon the above tests.

The five proposed criteria here (when applied to a conceptual layer of Truth) can be used as a mode of 'triangulation' wherein the more of them apply to a proposed layer, the more likely that proposition is in fact a stand alone layer.

This method of analysis can be used when attempting to identify layers of Truth. Although this method of triangulating construct validity only extends to individual layers, it doesn't extend to qualifying whatever constructs you may create out of them. That will be a function that becomes more demonstrable once a number of layers have been categorized (and subsequently organized in relation to each other) to produce a functional, proprietary construct that can then be more empirically tested in its own right.

Now, let's carry on to the next question considering layers; "Is there overlap between layers?". This is a deceptively critical question. Its depth in concept has as much to do with whether or not there is overlap as it does with what kind of overlap is in question.

If we were considering the overlap of individual true things within different layers (or Truth fragments), then the answer is yes. It's not impossible, or even uncommon, to find something that is true in one layer to also be true within another. This is most common the more directly proximal a layer is with another. This is also one of the aspects of layers that makes it possible for malicious actors to fool people into false conclusions or incorrect perceptions. By using something that is true at different layers, they can covertly switch the layer within their story that may seem to justify a faulty conclusion.

If, instead, the question is regarding the possibility of layers overlapping other layers (or Truth fragments), then the answer can also be yes, but in a much more interesting way than you may think. If you conceptualize layers of Truth fragments as a stratified, vertical column, the overlap would appear complete. A congruency of ordered, harmonious strata from the bottom to the top. But if you consider that each complete layer is composed of a myriad of true things regarding it, you'll recall that it's the difference and not the similarity between the total Truth of a layer that differentiates it from another. So in this sense, were you to situate sequential layers vertically, they would be offset of each other by the degree of difference between their constituent true things. In that way, a vertical tower may look more like a zig-zag than a column. Each strata as close as a single true thing apart or as different as only one true thing in relation.

Some of the ancient beliefs we are going to explore in later chapters consider the connection of all layers of Truth as universally fractal from top to bottom. That is to say that a unifying chord connects every layer from the highest to the lowest strata of total Truth. There's another possibility to the connection of layers than that of a tower. This type of construct, though still harmonious with the idea of a unifying chord, is less linear but fractal in its own right.

In the practice of neuroscience, the human brain was discovered to be the culmination of an innumerable amount of connections that makes up a network known as a neural net. This network was proposed as early as 1873 by Scottish philosopher and empiricist Alexander Bain. What this model presents is not a linear tower of derivative strata, but a galaxy of interconnected nodes. Though the entire structure of the network is finite (it's all constrained within the brain), the construct itself presents a phenomenally complex architecture that functions more as a multifaceted symphony than a linear directory. This model has been expropriated from biology into the algorithmic constructs of artificial intelligence and computer learning. The philosophy of a neural net is, in fact, an apt structure to represent what each of our limited perspectives of total reality are like. Not everyone has the same nodes in their system. Or the same connections, or as many of either in comparison. This, itself, is a fractal image within differing layers of what it is to be a human being.

Conceptually, I leave open the possibility that total Truth could exist as a unified whole within a universe of interconnected layers. Each within their clusters and galaxies of similarity and interconnectivity. Some layers more tightly connected than others, yet all of them are bound within the same total network of emmet.

Were this the case, it would speak much more broadly to the possibility of proprietary constructs of reality that we each wind up building internally within the whole of the network. The complexity would be untold orders of magnitude beyond enumerating the keys on a hypothetical piano. Although, admittedly, that kind of network would be quite difficult (if not impossible) to validate by way of construct validation simply due to the enormous grandeur of such a lattice.

The final question raised regarding qualifying layers was, "How do you distinguish layers apart, one from another?". Though this was implicitly answered within the definition process of what layers are themselves, it's distinct enough from the question of overlap that I'll make it explicit for its own sake.

At least three out of the five criteria for identifying a layer that were laid out above will aid specifically in the process of differentiation between adjoining layers. Those are:

- A layer can be intuitively distinct without significant explanation.

In many cases (particularly those where two layers are either separated by significant breadth of scale or difference in concept), the distinction of layers is an intuitive matter of fact.

- An action applied to proposed layers that are considered related, or proximal in concept, produces differing results.

This can be a very empirical manner by which to distinguish the separation between layers. If you're trying to figure out where sequential layers bifurcate, a logical separation would include enough distinction between layers to affect a different outcome from the same action applied to each.

- Adjusting the scope or scale of a known layer reveals different layers based upon the above tests.

This final heuristic is one that seems as reliable and consistent as the principle of intuitive distinction. Truth fragments seem to exist within defined strata that don't follow (in their entirety) when scaling up, down, or away from the layer in question. As you do that, the peripheral layers surrounding it begin to make themselves self-evident by the aforementioned five criteria of layer distinction.

THE THREE PILLARS OF PERCEPTION

In my previous book, *Consciousness Reality & Purpose*, I spoke about three pillars that I consider vital to the building of any well balanced worldview. They are, in effect, three differing vantages from which you may view any given concept. Though all three can be called upon to answer a given question, the uniqueness of their tact finds each of them better suited for certain questions than either of the other two. Those three pillars are: the scientific, the philosophic, and the theologic.

The scientific pillar is best suited for questions that are more founded within the material, empirical layers of reality. Things that can be objectively quantified by universal criteria that lead to predictable, repeatable results. The realms of physics and the natural sciences fall squarely beneath the purview of the scientific pillar. Everything material can most readily be known through the sciences.

The philosophic pillar is best suited for those cognitive thoughts and immaterial concepts that stem broadly from within the minds of men. Social, psychological, and epistemological questions and concepts rest comfortably atop the pillar of philosophy. Though often complimentary to the pillar of science, the rigorous constraints that bind science firmly within its bounds are less restrictive within philosophy. Questions that have no answers and concepts that have no application within the material world are still acceptable and even commonplace in philosophy. Though the presence of logic is still a prerequisite within a philosophic framework, one is permitted to meander beyond the boundaries of the empirical.

The theologic pillar is best suited for every layer of reality and Truth that cannot be adequately quantified by science or qualified by philosophy. The immeasurably broad range of the total Truth necessarily extends beyond the possible reach of both of the previous pillars. How far beyond is an impossible thing to know. In this sense, though the theological pillar relies the least upon objective qualification, it may theoretically represent the largest portion of the total Truth. That which is beyond our ability to dissect or predict leaves the pillars of science and philosophy wanting. The most valuable and unique quality of the theologic pillar that gives it such incredible utility in comparison to the other two is that of faith. Faith — the allowance to believe in something that cannot be known is considered by philosophy (at the least), foolish; and by the sciences (at the most), anathema. But if a large portion of total reality (and by nature, total Truth) cannot be known by man in his finite quality, the only hope that remains for him is faith in the unknown. This is the purpose and the strength of the theologic pillar.

Were I to conceptualize the three pillars in their relation to each other (even as layers in their own rights), I would place philosophy in-between science and theology. It acts as a mediator that spans and joins the most material concepts with the most ethereal ones. Being that our default vantage point is that of a human being, with all of the limitations and considerations that entails, the human mind is the sandbox from which we can stretch out one direction (into the material) and its opposite (into the ethereal). In that sense, you could even conceptualize the three pillars (instead of separate modalities) as a continuous spectrum or corridor. Where on the far end are the sciences that blend towards the middle (the philosophical) and then continue to the other end towards the theological. We, as humans, are stationed in the middle and can venture in either direction based upon our questions as well as our proclivities.

This construct (the three pillars) is how I will be structuring the major portions of this book. The next three chapters will represent the majority of our exploration into the Truth. The first will be Truth in science. The second, Truth in Philosophy. The third will look at Truth in theology.

All within the landscape of discovering layers of Truth in each. How they've been used, misused, and organized by man in his attempts to rationalize his extraordinary existence amidst the unfathomably vast universe of emmet.

CHAPTER II

TRUTH IN SCIENCE

"It's easier to fool people than it is to convince them they have been fooled."

— MARK TWAIN

2

TRUTH IN SCIENCE

"Science is a way of thinking much more than it is a body of knowledge"

— CARL SAGAN

The world in which I write this is a technological one. One that is inundated, even over-saturated, by mechanical and electronic marvels that would boggle the minds of our ancient forebears. The generations that have been born into and inherited the bounty of 21st century technology are the heirs to thousands of years of human striving in the sciences.

Of all three pillars, the scientific is the one responsible for the majority of all tangible, material progress that humanity has made over the millennia. Miraculous inventions of engineering and real world problem solving have built the throne of prominence that science has been seated upon for at least 200 years. We now find ourselves as the wealthy benefactors of the many discoveries, and their implementations, that define our age.

Even though this is the position we hold due to the power of science in action, as this pillar has been hyper-focused upon, its predominance over the other two has caused a bloating within its hallowed halls that has lead to corruption and rot.

I start with this pillar among the three, partly because it is the most universally recognized in our society. Partly because it has the most obvious affects within it. But partly because it has become so trusted in its ubiquity that society has become myopic to its faults, limits, and snakes within.

I, admittedly, may come across as the most critical of this pillar out of the three. In this present age, I see what amounts to a monolith where a triumvirate should reside. And in the monarchical status it holds above society, its dictates and prescriptions create wide reaching and deeply affecting shock waves that carry significant weight behind each. Many of them lead to prosperity. But many others create suffering.

Suffering not only in the corporal sense, but in the cognitive and spiritual spheres it overshadows by its eminence.

The spirit of science is one of unencumbered Truth. The scientific process is a framework that's meant to hone in on what is reliably true about anything that can be tested. But that spirit has been ossified into a totem, an idol. Man, in his hubris, has situated himself as the steward of science. But as the translator of its spirit, has injected all of the shortcomings of a person whose other two vital pillars have atrophied from neglect.

My aim in this chapter is to unearth the unadulterated spirit of the scientific. Its history, both good and bad. The strength that its light brings to man when followed with deference and attention. And the monstrous horror it can inflict when mismanaged, misrepresented, or idolized.

The Truth of science can be a powerful blade that cuts both ways. And lies, in the name of science, can be a cancer that grows within a society that is ignorant of those within it who feed it.

Science, as most people perceive it today, is a process by which ideas can be functionally qualified or disqualified through rigorous and repeatable testing. The basic process, that we all learned in grade school, starts with an observation which becomes a hypothesis. That hypothesis is tested and re-tested, by researchers and their peers, in an effort to disprove it as true. If, after sufficient attempts to disprove the hypothesis, all efforts fail to do so and instead produce a repeatable, predictable outcome; the hypothesis becomes a working theory.

Really, in science, that's about as high of a standing as one can hope for. Theories can further be instantiated as laws or principals, but one thing you won't ever hear an honest scientist call a theory is a fact.

This is considered to be, perhaps, the most laudable function of good science. The idea that any idea — be they considered theory, principal, or law — can in fact, be wrong. When it so happens that a recognized theory in the scientific practice has been found lacking, or even faulty, that accepted theory will either be amended or scrapped altogether in place of a more functional one. This is considered science "self correcting" or "improving over time".

With this as a guiding dictate and flexible backbone to rely upon, man has been granted the ability to prove what he can, as best he can. And if what has been proven is later disproven, that is seen as a net positive, something to be celebrated.

THE EMPIRICAL MODEL

Perhaps the most useful tool in the scientific method is something called *empiricism*. If something is empirically proven or considered empirically correct it is given scientific credence as a functional model. But, what exactly is empiricism and why is it so heavily relied upon by the sciences?

Empiricism could be traced back as far as 600 BCE in schools of Hindu thought, but what is seen primarily in science these days is a descendant of what could more distinctly be called British empiricism. The forebears of this practice were philosophers such as Francis Bacon and Thomas Hobbes. Their ideas, that became what we now know as empirical science, stemmed from the assertion that true knowledge can only come by way of our sensory experience. In other words, our five major senses are the only barometer of what is real that can be trusted.

So if someone were to say that something was empirically true, that means it has been tested in a method related to its observable, material traits that can be quantified and qualified by our own senses. This, by definition, leaves out any hypotheses that hold only within the philosophically hypothetical. Even the mathematically theoretical wouldn't be considered empirically true until a test of its legitimacy could be formulated and passed in the material world and not just on a chalkboard.

In that way, empiricism could be defined as its own layer of Truth within the scientific pillar. Though not the only one (rationalism would be its opposing counterpart that considers reason as the chief avenue to knowledge), it's certainly the layer that is most well known when the scientific is considered by most.

On a broader scale (one that's not confined only to the scientific), the material could be considered the most accessible of all layers of reality to us as humans who exist so physically and cognitively bound within it. So it shouldn't come as any surprise that we are not only the most reliant upon our discoveries regarding it, but most trust that which we can qualify by way of our universal senses.

With such a fundamental, utilitarian basis for finding and testing the material world around us, the societies of modernity have become very comfortable trusting that which this branch of science presents to us by way of vetted theories. And why should they not? Were a theory found to be inaccurate, faulty, or incorrect, it would be amended through that reliable function of self correction, would it not?

Like every other hypothesis that gets presented and tested through the empirical, scientific method, the method itself appears flawless on paper. But since it's been implemented within total reality as a form of Truth qualifier, what has played out in the material world fades in comparison to the hypothetical version of it that we were taught to trust.

THE DEMON IN THE METHOD

One of the natural limitations of being human is the finite duration of our individual existences. How can a singular person be expected to learn, by themselves, all of the Truth that they need to know before they die? Our mortality has always been a thorn in the side of our progress towards learning more about any given fragment of Truth.

But we, as a collective, in contrast to the individual, have discovered a workaround that can defy our mortality. The transmission of knowledge through succeeding generations grants passage for humanity as a whole to tempt immortality in the face of our individual demise. One of the most famous empiricists of all time, Sir Isaac Newton, is quoted as saying, "If I have seen further, it is by standing on the shoulders of giants.".

You could look at this as a functional benefit to the difference between layers of humanity. In the case of knowledge transmission, what is true as an individual (the limitations of what can personally be discovered) doesn't follow to the layer of communal humanity. The dynamics between these two layers of Truth are actually quite fascinating and will be a subject that we come back to in many instances.

It's within this layer of reality that, for all we gain from its utility, we simultaneously on-board a new detriment that is as unique to it as it is inevitable. Because what is generally missing at the level of the meta-empirical (that which we presume is being played out in reality) is a variable that is innate to we who do the testing. Humans, at the level of the communal, invoke the presence of a demon that corrupts and rots all of man's systems. And it does so, not by dint of the system itself, but for the presence of man within it.

In 2014, philosopher Scott Alexander wrote a now famous essay titled *"Meditations on Moloch"*. In this lengthy and incisive indictment of human systems, Alexander begins with a poem by the 20th century American poet Allen Ginsburg on the demon, Moloch. The poem reads as such:

What sphinx of cement and aluminum bashed open their skulls and ate up their brains and imagination?

Moloch! Solitude! Filth! Ugliness! Ashcans and unobtainable dollars! Children screaming under the stairways! Boys sobbing in armies! Old men weeping in the parks!

Moloch! Moloch! Nightmare of Moloch! Moloch the loveless! Mental Moloch! Moloch the heavy judger of men!

Moloch the incomprehensible prison! Moloch the crossbone soulless jailhouse and Congress of sorrows! Moloch whose buildings are judgment! Moloch the vast stone of war! Moloch the stunned governments!

Moloch whose mind is pure machinery! Moloch whose blood is running money! Moloch whose fingers are ten armies! Moloch whose breast is a cannibal dynamo! Moloch whose ear is a smoking tomb!

Moloch whose eyes are a thousand blind windows! Moloch whose skyscrapers stand in the long streets like endless Jehovahs! Moloch whose factories dream and croak in the fog! Moloch whose smokestacks and antennae crown the cities!

Moloch whose love is endless oil and stone! Moloch whose soul is electricity and banks! Moloch whose poverty is the specter of genius! Moloch whose fate is a cloud of sexless hydrogen! Moloch whose name is the Mind!

Moloch in whom I sit lonely! Moloch in whom I dream Angels! Crazy in Moloch! Cocksucker in Moloch! Lacklove and manless in Moloch!

Moloch who entered my soul early! Moloch in whom I am a consciousness without a body! Moloch who frightened me out of my natural ecstasy! Moloch whom I abandon! Wake up in Moloch! Light streaming out of the sky!

Moloch! Moloch! Robot apartments! invisible suburbs! skeleton treasuries! blind capitals! demonic industries! spectral nations! invincible madhouses! granite cocks! monstrous bombs!

They broke their backs lifting Moloch to Heaven! Pavements, trees, radios, tons! lifting the city to Heaven which exists and is everywhere about us!

Visions! omens! hallucinations! miracles! ecstasies! gone down the American river!

Dreams! adorations! illuminations! religions! the whole boatload of sensitive bullshit!

Breakthroughs! over the river! flips and crucifixions! gone down the flood! Highs! Epiphanies! Despairs! Ten years' animal screams and suicides! Minds! New loves! Mad generation! down on the rocks of Time!

Real holy laughter in the river! They saw it all! the wild eyes! the holy yells! They bade farewell! They jumped off the roof! to solitude! waving! carrying flowers! Down to the river! into the street!

In Ginsburg's apocryphal curse, the personified, demonic specter of Moloch is the poetic representative of an ancient pagan god that goes back to the Carthaginian era and is interchangeable within a number of pantheons in that time with the god Ba'al.

In those ancient and barbaric times, Moloch was worshiped in the form of a brazen half-bull, half-man. It is said that followers would sacrifice living children to Moloch, as a sign of something they hold most dear, on the promise of some form of prescribed bounty. A rainy season, a bountiful harvest, victory in war. A sacrifice of cherished innocence for an otherwise inaccessible benefit.

In both the poem above and Alexander's essay citing it, Moloch is presented as a philosophical demon instead of a metaphysical one. Moloch, in this sense, represents the tendency that any human systems have to become a race-to-the-bottom that cannot be avoided and that leads to the utter corruption of it for man's sake. It's a function that doesn't rely on the majority within the system, but instead perpetuates from the least moral people within it.

If you were to transpose the idea of child sacrifices to the brazen image of Moloch within a modern human system, the child represents a personal moral or ethic that someone is willing to sacrifice for some prescribed benefit of doing so. In the economic sense (Alexander illuminated), within a tightly contested industry, the benefit of cheating (sacrificing a moral or ethic) for some, outweigh the possible detriment of getting caught for doing so. In that way, anyone who is willing to make the necessary sacrifice will jump to the front of the pack.

What's worse, this creates pressure upon the rest of those within the same industry to either also sacrifice those morals to stay in the race or retain their morality at the cost of getting steamrolled and relegated into obscurity.

It's a form of evolutionary pressure where the mutation of the norm, so long as it offers a superior advantage, will wind up taking over the population by way of its fitness in comparison to the previous iteration.

This is Moloch. This is the *race to the bottom*. And it's impossible to prevent.

Given enough time, man becomes the disease that cripples and disables the most perfect of systems. No matter if 99.99% of people within the system uphold its values, the most selfish or self-interested 0.01% wind up corrupting the entire endeavor.

Even within a system that is ostensibly thought to be an objective one like empiricism, because it is driven by, overseen by, and qualified by people; Moloch pervades.

As remarkably adaptive and inventive as mankind is in the discovery and creation of systems and sciences, it is also by these same qualities that we are so well suited to devising ways of circumventing the safeguards of them all. Given enough time and enough people within a system, man — by way of Moloch — will twist what was into whatever best suits himself.

THE HEIST OF HISTORY

To those who revere and hold empirical science as an impenetrable fortress, one that has the benefit of objectivity and the inherent mechanism of self correction, you may feel the pangs of critique assailing your sensibilities. So far what I've alleged, itself, is nothing more than hypothetical. Where is the critical proof for this kind of accusation?

I will, for exactly this reason, cite a number of examples that are not only easily verifiable but are only a short tally among an ever repeating cycle of similar follies that persist in this predictable way.

But before I do, there is more that needs to be laid out.

Examples of failure and corruption of the scientific process is just the *'what'*. If Moloch is the *'why'*, what is the *'how'* that allows humanity at a communal level to *race to the bottom* by way of the minority that precipitates a false reality to the majority by their actions?

The answer is a simple one. And it's one that we've already covered. For two reasons, man's understanding (even his understanding of the systems he's produced and considers removed from himself) are only ever partial (at best) and corrupted (at worst).

The first is because, as laid out in the introduction, even the totality of man's understanding is necessarily incomplete due to our insignificant total understanding of emmet. Though (through the mechanism of empirical science) we may add to and correct that which exists at any point within human understanding, the totality of it is like a proprietary network that exists as a bubble of what's presently known amidst a sea of what entirely is. By this limitation alone, the best we can ever hope for is a system that meets most of our needs at the material level of Truth that we primarily work within. While at the same time, with all humility, understand that we almost certainly don't correctly understand what we think we do by the inevitable omission of all that we do not (and, perhaps, cannot) know. Anyone under these preconditions who believes they have a grasp on even the complete understanding of that single layer of Truth is already living in a false reality.

The second part of the 'how', that permits access for those who would sacrifice their morals to Moloch to dement empiricism for their benefit, is the thing that people are the best at — story.

Remember, there is a filter that exists (and cannot be avoided) between raw data and our understanding or transmission thereof. We, as the vector of translation, must interpret what we see (even from the emotionless heart of empirical information) into story. Narrative. Something that gives the data meaning and importance. We cannot parse data for data's sake. It must hold significance. And that significance doesn't come as part of the information itself. It's incumbent upon those doing the studies and tests to follow the process to its conclusion, and then translate the results into whatever they believe the story is that they tell.

Perhaps one of the most commonly used, cited, and easily corruptible methods of doing this is through the field of statistics.

British prime minister Benjamin Disraeli is cited as first saying a line that was later made famous by American writer Mark Twain. There are "Lies, damned lies, and statistics". Statistical analysis, and the job of statisticians in general, is to formulate visual meaning from large gatherings of specific data. Typically rendered in spread sheets, pie charts, and line graphs; they are relied upon by nearly every other field of science as an empirical barometer of effect within a system, or group of intersecting systems.

Colloquially speaking, the majority of mankind looks at statistics as akin to facts. Little do most people know just how subjectively arbitrary statistics can be. All due to the very same reasons we've already covered. The outcomes are entirely and necessarily predicated upon the framework of the test, the accuracy of the data, the completeness of the data, and the moral fortitude of those involved.

Even within a culture of peer review and reputable journals that are meant to hold all findings to the highest level of scrutiny, Moloch can (and does) seep in through the cracks of academia and typically seeds its folly in the fertile soil of the statistical.

You don't even need to outright lie to cause a statistical finding to lead to the result you wanted it to to begin with. By carefully shaping of what data is allowed in and what is specifically kept out, the correct results of a statistical review can produce a false reality that is utterly opposed to the actual Truth.

Not to lay the entire burden of evil upon the single field of statistics, the same sorts of chicanery can be played out in other avenues of the empirical scientific endeavor. Any sort of test, or trial, that is proposed to implore the great scalpel of empiricism depends entirely upon the veracity of its construction.

The sad truth of the matter is that the effects of Moloch in so many branches of science over so many years and for so many different reasons have led us to a point in time where scientific findings can be willfully falsified, and those that are supposed to safeguard such actions aren't merely ignorant to them, but sometimes — complicit.

When man is the arbiter of what is true — even when supposedly implementing the machinations of an objective process — who else is there to oversee the overseer? The real world outcome of this corrosive pathology within the most highly revered beacon of light and Truth in our modern age has bred nothing short of catastrophe.

WHEN SCIENCE GOES WRONG

The time has come now to present some actual, verifiable examples of these happenings within this, our most trusted pillar. If the implicit explanations of the *'why'* and the *'how'* aren't convincing enough, then the following explicit examples of *'what'* should leave no questions left in your mind.

In order to understand these examples, one must first have a sense of how the structures of science work in the real world. I don't mean the pure, analytical methodology. I mean how the process of discovery, recognition, and final acceptance within academia works. Because the ability to skew and corrupt what we, as a communal super-intelligence reliant upon those at the forefront of each field to add to our immortal body of knowledge, accept as true is largely due to the gaming and deceptions that have captured this process.

The first thing that needs to be made explicitly clear is that, functionally speaking, progress in any field of science only (and necessarily) happens at the fringes. It relies upon the heretical heterodox. The out-of-the-box thinkers. Those willing to offend the orthodoxy of their time with counter-narratives. If the greatest strength of science comes from its ability to change its story and adjust it with better explanations, every new addition (and thus progression) comes from outside of accepted science.

Were this process happening in a vacuum, devoid of human considerations, it would function seamlessly. But since humans are not only within the system but are all of the vital arbitrators along the process, the messiness of humanity greatly affects the outcome of the system itself. One thing that has historically been axiomatic of humanity is the desire for and abuse of archetypal power. We glean much of our self-worth from the eminence others grant us based upon their perception of our deserving it. Once we've been given prominence and power, we are bitterly loath to give it up.

If your identity (and by extension, your self-worth) is contingent upon the continuation of eminence granted by your peers, any threat that may relinquish you of it will be fought against tooth and nail. In this way, those that progressed the sciences at the fringe (the heterodox) became the new, accepted science (the orthodox). And — in all irony — the orthodox is prototypically antagonistic to the heterodox, even though it's what permitted them to become the orthodox themselves.

This diametric tension between these two competing forces should present a predictable dance. Something that looks like two steps forward and one step back. That's still progress. But only within a system where the orthodoxy can be questioned and tested fairly. When outside, foreign interests reinforce the orthodoxy, a wholesale stagnation can occur that, from the outside, looks like the proving of the status quo. Where, in reality, it's a synthetic and highly manipulated false reality that's being propped up to benefit those in power — both in the positions of eminence within the orthodoxy and those who benefit from it remaining instantiated.

The logical and responsible answer to this conundrum is to create oversight mechanisms. Gatekeepers all throughout the process. Something that is separate and unencumbered by any bias or slight-of-hand within the orthodoxy. To create regulators.

The problem with this solution is the very same problem that required a solution in the first place. Humans constitute the entire apparatus built to regulate the other human driven apparatuses. In the same way and for similar reasons, those stop-gates meant to prevent corruption of the academic scientific process can themselves become corrupted; captured.

It's become so ubiquitous and pathogenic within every kind of human system that it requires little in the way of explanation beyond the term that defines it: regulatory capture. In the cog-works of industry, that can be at the level of health, safety, or ethics regulators. In the academies, it can be at the level of peer-review or eminent dynasties. Whatever body or process gets erected to combat intrinsic corruption, given enough time for Moloch to work, will wind up becoming the very implement used to fool a willing public into a belief in science falsely so-called.

A PROBLEM WITH THE BRAIN

Our first historically verifiable example of an orthodoxological atrocity takes us back to the 1930s. And to be able to transpose yourself into the culture of the time will require a certain degree of understanding of the scientific landscape that under-pinned it.

Being only a few decades removed from the 1800s, much of the medical understanding — the giants whose shoulders were being stood upon — stemmed from this period of history. In fact, within the early 1900s, the entire practice of psychology (and psychiatry by extension) was the newest form of science that was recently accepted as credible. It was very much in its infancy. Most of those pushing it forward into academic credibility were, by necessity, those heterodox thinkers. Before it was accepted by the sciences, psychiatrists were considered more of a pseudo-scientific ilk and went by the term *alienists*.

It's within this 'wild west' form of what is much more instantiated now as a respectable science that anyone who could enthrone themselves as the scientific orthodoxy had a nascent field in which to do so.

You would think that this is the most likely point in a burgeoning field for incorrect conclusions to be accepted, and you'd be right. What's interesting about that though is that within such a vacuous body of work, you would think that correction would be much easier and quicker considering the unlikelihood of coming to a majority of true conclusions so early. The orthodoxy should be changing rapidly at the beginning of the journey of discovery if the scientific method is functioning smoothly.

What we find instead is an infamous cautionary tale of medical pseudoscience gone awry in what amounted to a mass mutilation that is looked back upon with righteous disdain and ire.

At this time, psychological asylums were a normal part of society. Not necessarily because psychoses were more common than they are now, but because there were very few that were treatable by the medical industry of the day. So, for lack of out-patient treatment options, those of a mentally ill disposition would be corralled in these facilities.

In 1935, Portuguese neurologist Egas Moniz attempted a novel treatment option on one such patient in a Lisbon hospital. Inspired by the experimental psychosurgical work of 1880s alienist Gottlieb Burckhardt, Moniz performed a neurosurgical intervention he called a "leucotomy". In this procedure, he drilled holes into the skull of the mentally unwell patient and injected pure alcohol onto the frontal lobe of their brain; destroying all the nerves and tissues it contacted.

What he recorded after this intervention was a remarkable reduction in the symptoms and presentation of the mental affliction that plagued the patient before then. His empirical, scientific success was the first in his field that boasted the possibility of societal reintegration for the mentally insane. Thus reducing the overpopulation of the asylum systems while simultaneously reducing the danger these people posed to the public and themselves.

Moniz would later win the Nobel prize in medicine for this innovation in 1949.

One year after Moniz's breakthrough, American neuroscientist Jackson Freeman would adopt the leucotomy and wind up renaming it the "lobotomy".

Carrying on the work of his Portuguese colleague, Freeman (with the help of a neurosurgeon named James Watts) would further innovate on the procedure and, instead of using alcohol, began to use a tool modeled after an ice-pick, called a "leucotome" to sever the frontal lobes of his patients by piercing it through their eye sockets. It allowed for a relatively quick procedure that left no scars.

Lobotomies would be heralded as the pinnacle of the psychiatric sciences for decades after its inception. Used to treat conditions as extreme as schizophrenia and as benign as chronic depression. It was widely considered a sort of physiological 'reset' of an ill brain. And since the patients were objectively freed from their manias after the intervention, it became very nearly a fad between the 1940s and 1960s.

But a nagging criticism hounded the practice of lobotomies. Critics protested the procedure from the heterodoxical fringes saying that you aren't treating the condition so much as you're preempting the physical possibility of it being manifested. Those lobotomized patients were simply physically unable to express their psychosis while we on the outside considered them cured of it altogether. Akin to fixing the problem of a 'check engine' light by disconnecting the circuit that caused it to light up.

What's more, this was far from an exact science. Anecdotal cases started piling up of patients who did not improve from it, got worse from it, or even died as a result of it. These cases were broadly dismissed as a possible side effect of what was otherwise a marvel of modern medicine. One that made the careers and reputations of highly regarded trailblazers of their time. Those who protested lobotomies as unnecessary, ineffective, or morally abominable were eschewed as foolish or antithetical to the progress of medical science. There was little to no oversight in the industry at this point and, as such, to contravene the orthodoxy meant a direct affront to the monolithic heroes of their field. The hopes of changing their minds from the inside of science by appealing to their faulty conclusions were a lost cause.

It took a very public incident to occur, that created a cultural wave of abject indignation for the practice, before lobotomies would not only fall out of fad but become seen as abhorrently cruel.

That incident occurred relatively early in the history of the procedure, in 1940, when it was given to Rosemary Kennedy, the sister of future American president John F. Kennedy. Rosemary presented with a mental impairment early in life. She was slow learning to crawl, slow to learn to walk, and even slower to pick up speech. She would be capable of participating in family activities and even kept a diary in her teen years. But by the age of 22, her family said she didn't show signs of progressing and, worryingly, started to show signs of going backwards.

Jackson Freeman himself would end up suggesting and performing the lobotomy on Rosemary Kennedy. Afterwards, though, she became permanently incapacitated and barely able to function.

She would become known in the public zeitgeist decades later as the poster child for what would become the Special

Olympics, an event that was founded by Rosemary's younger sister, Eunice Kennedy Shriver, in 1962. At this point, nearly 30 years after the first leucotomy was performed, the public began to sour to the whole procedure. Seeing it as barbaric and inhumane.

In the first two decades after it was considered scientific orthodoxy to lobotomize the mentally ill, an estimated 60,000 Americans had their frontal lobes destroyed in this manner. The sciences didn't correct over time. It took the outrage of the masses to shame the orthodoxy away from what they considered worthy of a Nobel prize not too long before.

In 1950, the Soviet Union became the first country in the world to expressly ban the practice on the grounds that it was "contrary to the principles of humanity". Other countries, like Japan and Germany, would soon follow suit.

In 1967, Jackson Freeman would be banned from ever performing another lobotomy after one of his patients suffered a fatal brain hemorrhage by his hands.

Lobotomies were never banned outright in the United States, and the practice continued into the 1980s. Though they are rarely performed anymore, they are not expressly illegal in the country where they were popularized.

SMOKE AND MIRRORS

If you were born in the late 1990s or early 2000s, you may not even recognize the controversy and wholesale capture of industry, government, media, and science that happened in the century prior. A monumental exercise in psychological, institutional, and cultural take over that was greatly empowered through and propped up by the manipulation of science.

The story starts back near the turn of the 20th century, long before any regulatory stop-gates would come into effect in this area. Long before society in general even realized there was any need for them to.

In 1910, the American tobacco industry was producing 10 billion cigarettes annually, and by 1930, they would be producing 123 billion cigarettes annually. How? With an injection of marketing savvy plus the use of shrewd psychological science.

Both the magic of marketing and the science of psychology that allowed for this industry to twelve times its size in twenty years was due almost entirely to one man — Edward Bernays.

Bernays was a 25 year old Austrian born Jew who, in 1917, applied to fight in the First World War for America. Fatefully, he would be summarily denied entry into the armed forces on account of his poor eye sight and flat feet. Intent on serving his country in some sort of tangential capacity, he applied to work for the US Committee of Public Information. A relatively new bureaucracy whose goal was the curation of public perception at home to raise the morale of the people towards the war effort. If you were to put it in Orwellian terms, the CPI was the US Ministry of Truth. Stated plainly, it was the American government's propaganda machine.

Edward would organize rallies and produce propaganda posters to bolster support for the war from home. He did such a phenomenal job in this regard that, after the war was won, President Woodrow Wilson would personally invite Bernays to join him at the signing of the Paris peace accord in France.

With all he had learned during the war, Bernays realized he had honed a powerful tool. One that could be used to convince massive amounts of people that anything is true. As such, he set out to put it to work for him in the newly booming American market place. Through successful advertisement campaigns in the food industry, by the 1920s, he had gained legendary status in the advertising world rite large.

In 1929, Bernays was approached by the tobacco industry with a proposition that was right up his alley. Up until that point, cigarette companies had done a remarkable job getting the male population in America hooked on their products. But the way they did that was by building a strong cultural relationship between said products and a masculine image. That was all well and good if all they wanted were male customers, but it naturally excluded half of the potential market by default. If there was a way to convince women to also smoke cigarettes (which was a cultural faux pas due to their tie to masculinity) then they could double their sales overnight.

With this goal in his cross-hairs, Edward quickly identified the issue of the masculine image and sought to rectify it. What he identified at the same time was a deeply rooted psychological truism about the social perceptions of human beings.

We, as individuals, are apt to put trust in those we either look up to as avatars of who we aspire to be or in those we hold as figures of authority. The way to cause a mass of people to emulate an action is to present an idol, or figment of desire, that portrays that action favorably.

In that time, in American pop culture, the women's suffrage movement was a popular cause among the female cohort of the country. Women were seen as folk heroes when they worked to take their power back from men. One of the biggest cultural events of the day was the New York City Easter Day parade. In this annual event, women of the upper class would wear their finest attire and walk down the city streets to the adoration of every other woman watching from the sidelines. Bernays decided this was his way into the zeitgeist. In the 1929 Easter Day parade, he paid many upper-class women to wear clothes that were nice but not too nice, and while walking in plain view of the masses, they all light up cigarettes in defiance of the norm.

By very publicly displaying avatars of desire, who were wearing clothes that may be within reach for many of the middle class, he presented idols for those women of the common folk to emulate. An image of rebellion and power. Of freedom from the patriarchal grip of the masculine. Bernays would use that image in advertisement and called it "Torches for Freedom".

Needless to say, the effect took off in popular culture and became a massive success and proof of concept for Bernays and (more specifically) for big tobacco as an industry.

But why does any of that specific history matter to the topic at hand? What does all this have to do with Truth in science? I laid all of that groundwork to prepare you for what brought on the next 70 years of mass manipulation by one of the world's most powerful industries. This was made possible by the money they'd made, Bernays' tactic of psychological emulation, and the addition of them together to use science as the reinforcement of a pseudo-reality.

In the mid 1900s, two landmark studies were released that absolutely rocked the tobacco industry to the core. In 1953 and 1964, studies from the president of the Cancer Society and the US Surgeon General respectively both proved incontrovertible links between smoking and cancer. Were this any other product at that time, it would have sounded the death tome for their industry. But, between what they had learned from Bernays in 1929 and a new, dedicated angle of attack on the academies of science directly, Big Tobacco declared war on reality for the next 45 years.

In the midst of those damning scientific studies, the advertisement campaigns shifted from making men feel manly and women feeling empowered to a focus on doctors directly. Endless television commercials, newspaper, and magazine ads showed general practitioners smoking and suggesting their patients do too. "More doctors prefer Lucky Strike!". These and ads like them appealed through the avatars of the very authorities that were damning their products as lethal.

And it worked! The general population didn't consume scientific studies. And if doctors seem to be promoting their addiction, then maybe cigarettes were actually healthy.

At the very same time that this public propaganda campaign swept the culture, a new official research organization (fully funded by Big Tobacco)

was born called the Council for Tobacco Research. Just this body alone, whose sole purpose was to overwhelm the scientific literature with beneficial papers, produced over 7,000 published studies that led to at least 10 different Nobel prizes for their work!

So whenever some person or organization would try to sue any tobacco company, they would be utterly avalanched in court with accepted science that obscured any claim they could possibly have of harm or wrongdoing.

This constructed a generations-long false reality where people who said smoking caused cancer were ridiculed as unscientific doomsayers.

By the year 2000, estimated cigarette related deaths in the US alone hit a staggering 450,000 deaths annually. That equates to over 1200 Americans dying per day — the equivalent of two jumbo airliners full of passengers crashing to the ground and killing everyone on board — every day of the year.

Late into the 1990s, the government and regulatory bodies would end up winning major lawsuits against the industry. But by then, the damage was done. It was fostered into generations worth of minds and fortified by decades of fake science. Once more, science didn't correct over time. The people had to be protected by an intervention outside of the Moloch corrupted academies.

Even though American tobacco users have declined from around 25% of the population in 1998 to about 15% in 2015, as of 2017, tobacco related illnesses are still the number one cause of death in the state of California.

THINK OF THE CHILDREN

If it hasn't become clear by this point, the problem with empirical science isn't exactly the process itself. It's the corruptibility of the process (by way of man's part in the system) paired with the illusion of the system being impartial by design, which compounds the perception that we know what we think we know at any given point.

In the case of lobotomies, what was actually happening inside the heads of those lobotomized was difficult to know as a casual observer. And if suspicions were raised by those laymen, they were roundly retorted by the scientific authorities of the day. While in the case of smoking, the illnesses that led to over 100 million deaths in the 1900s was a battle of correlation versus causation. And though that argument was effectively settled by the 1950s, it was obscured and perpetuated by a wholesale sacrificing of scientific ethics at a scale we had never seen before.

But what if something were to happen in the medical sciences that was overtly obvious? That caused horrific deformations of the human body. And what if it were happening to the most defenseless and innocent people of all — to children?

Surely something at that level of abject horror would be identified and ceased by the integrity of the scientific process. Wouldn't it? Well, yes, but actually no.

In 1956, a new drug was introduced in Germany that purported to be an easing agent for the woes of pregnancy. Claiming to help prevent insomnia and nausea from morning sickness. Thalidomide was released to the public to be used by pregnant women.

The requisite safety testing for such pharmaceuticals wasn't what we have these days, and no pregnant women were ever used in the testing process.

Mice were the only living test subjects used before it was released to pregnant women. In fact, the mice used weren't even pregnant themselves in the tests. What they tested for was general toxicity, which the mice seemed to pass with flying colors. (More on this in the next example)

Once released and available as an over-the-counter morning sickness drug, it would be adopted by 46 countries through 14 different pharmaceutical companies under 37 different trade names. While the following years were a booming success for the industry, advertisements would be used to get the word out that said things like the following: *"Distaval [thalidomide] can be given with complete safety to pregnant women and nursing mothers without adverse effect on mother or child ... Outstandingly safe Distaval has been prescribed for nearly three years in this country."*

Meanwhile, in only the first year following its release (1957), reports of abnormal pregnancies and births began to accrue within the population of women who were taking thalidomide. Stillbirths and miscarriages were alarmingly high among them. But that wasn't even the worst of it.

Many of the children who actually made it to birth came out with horrifying, heart-rending malformations. They would range from no digits on their hands or feet (or too many on either) to missing legs and/or arms to hands or feet where their shoulders or hips should have started.

Just one of these cases would be bad enough. But thousands and thousands of these tragic, disfigured children would be born. It wasn't until the end of 1961, four years after it first hit the market, that thalidomide would be pulled from the shelf.

According to figures posted by the UK not-for-profit *Thalidomide Trust*, in that time period, an estimated 100,000 unborn babies were affected by the drug. It's generally estimated that around 10,000 "thalidomide babies" were actually delivered. Approximately 3000 of them are still alive today, nearly 70 years later. In correspondence that was discovered years later, the company that brought it to market (Chemie Grunenthal) was aware of studies warning them of these horrific malformations. They ignored them for four years. The same length of time that the entire First World War was fought for.

Between the disability of their malformations and the pain they cause, even those who survive today are a sober reminder of one of the darkest examples of a false reality —

backed by science — that bore out unthinkable human suffering before the correction process kicked in.

OF MICE & MEN

The dystopias of the tobacco and thalidomide stories, broadly speaking, stem from the greed and indifference of the marketing side of scientific industries. Where the lobotomy example was one that existed before proper regulatory and peer review firewalls were erected and required for such procedures.

What about modern examples? Is there something that has still slipped through the cracks of all these preventative checks and balances?

The final example in this chapter is one from the 21st century that may be continuing even today. If the hypotheses this revelation propose are correct, it may account for a massive amount of modern pharmaceutical nightmares that have plagued humanity in first world countries for decades! And it's due almost entirely to the scientific, academic side of the process — not the corporate one.

Before the story itself can be unfolded, though, a certain amount of detail and attention must be given to the focus of cellular biology. Especially as it pertains to a function of cell reproduction or, more specifically, a mechanism that either permits or denies it.

In the body, there are (broadly) two kinds of cells. *Somatic* cells and *Germ* cells. Germ cells are those specialized cells meant for reproducing people into the next generation (namely the sperm and the ova cells), whereas somatic cells are every other kind of cell that instead reproduces (divides) themselves within *this* generation.

In 1961, American anatomist Leonard Hayflick discovered a curious characteristic of somatic animal cell lines. The ability for cells to divide themselves for the sake of repair was well known and empirically understood by this point. But Hayflick discovered something that no one before had recognized about that process; that it was limited.

When an individual cell line was observed, one could witness it divide itself over and over again. But, interestingly, at some point it would just stop. The process of cellular reproduction seemed to inexplicably end after a certain number of iterations. When tested over and over again with the same kinds of cells from the same animal, the limit was the same. This was hence termed the Hayflick limit. Before this point, scientists like Alexis Carrel considered somatic cells effectively immortal. Hayflick, unbeknownst to him at the time, had stumbled upon a cellular hint into senescence, otherwise known as aging.

It wasn't until the early 2000s, when exploration at the genetic level became more resolved, that a mechanism was discovered that could explain the Hayflick limit. With the use of cutting-edge technology that wasn't available in the time of Leonard Hayflick, geneticists noticed an oddly repeating pattern of genetic code at the very end of each chromosome. It didn't look like any other part of the genetic sequence due largely to its short, repetitive pattern. It was when this pattern was quantified over successive generations of the same cell line, that their function became clear. After each cell division, the next cell would have one less repeating code. It was a countdown!

After all of the repeating bits of code (later called telomeres) were whittled down through continuous cell division, the cell line would stop dividing. Like pulling tabs off the bottom of a garage sale poster until there are none left.

Once this was understood and empirically proven, a popular hypothesis was forwarded suggesting that the reason telomeres were necessary to impose a Hayflick limit for each cell was a natural way to prevent cancer in the body.

What cancer is is the unnecessary and unmitigated reproduction of a cell. Were a cell to become damaged in some way (take radiation as an example) that caused it to reproduce erratically, its line could only divide to the number of its remaining telomeres before it couldn't divide anymore. Thus stopping a cancerous growth in its tracks. This connection between repair and cancer is vitally important to the story that is about to unfold.

The following is a personal story told by evolutionary biologist Bret Weinstein on his brother Eric's podcast called The Portal.

In the early 2000s, a young (then, undergraduate) Bret Weinstein was taking a seminar on cellular biology where a graduate student (who was focusing on oncology — the study of cancers) brought up the connection between telomeres and cancer. The graduate student didn't make the connections that immediately struck Weinstein. One direction was the immediate connection between telomeres as a mechanism of tumor suppression (as was being suggested by this graduate student) and the phenomenon of the Hayflick limit. The second connection was a much more subtle and elegant observation that Bret had read about in a paper by the famous evolutionary biologist George Williams.

In this paper, Williams wrote about a multivariate genetic function called a *pleiotropy*. In genetics, a pleiotropy is when a singular gene can be expressed in two or more different traits when activated in the same organism. This paper defined a specific categorization of pleiotropy titled an *antagonistic pleiotropy*.

The antagonistic pleiotropy hypothesis (as it would be known from William's work) suggested that the evolutionary method of natural selection that drove a species' fitness over successive generations had a correlation between specific survival traits and the life span of any particular species. To understand what that means, you must first understand that there was a previous evolutionary correlation between the size of an animal and how long it would live. The smaller the animal — like a mouse — the shorter the lifespan. The larger the animal — like an elephant — the longer the lifespan. This was seen as a general rule of thumb for many years. What Williams wrote about was a curious observation (that had also been around in the evolutionary circles that understood this) where certain adaptations of some animals that made them more likely to live longer in the wild — like a shell on a turtle, or the ability of birds to fly away from predators — caused their lifespans to be longer than they should have been compared to other animals of a similar size. The antagonistic pleiotropy hypothesis suggested that this was due to natural selection's pressures upon genes that have pleiotropic effects where one outcome of the gene is good in early life and bad in late life or vice versa. And that those traits that were beneficial in early life would be preferred in animals who were shorter lived and those beneficial in late life would be preferred by animals that were longer lived.

Essentially, at the risk of personifying evolution, natural selection could "see" species better depending on where the accumulation of their beneficial pleiotropic effects were within their lifespans. Therefore, selecting for the fittest of their lineage based upon those criteria.

What Weinstein recognized (between the connection of Hayflick's and Williams' works) was that the lifespans of animals (as defined through the antagonistic pleiotropy hypothesis) *must* present a mirror selection upon the length of telomeres as defined both by the size of the animal and their implicit or unique survival traits (ie: shells, wings, venom, etc.). This would be the most likely outcome that one would expect if a mouse and a bird of the same size had very different lifespans in comparison. Since the mouse's lifespan was shorter on average than the bird's (due to the bird's unique ability to prevent predation by flying away), the bird's telomeres should be longer than the mouse's by natural selection.

It seemed like a clear-cut and obvious hypothesis for Weinsein to test. And so he did, by digging into the recently expanding literature on animal telomere length. Starting with the most commonly tested model animal in laboratories — mice.

What he quickly discovered, though, would run absolutely afoul of this hypothesis in a way that would either fully discredit it or something far worse. He found out, from the literature, that mice had extraordinarily long telomeres. Not slightly long. Not very long. *Unbelievably* long. Something in the range of 10 times the length of the average human's telomeres!

This didn't seem to make sense. Bret would spend the next while trying to discover if there was some sort of academic error with this literature. Perhaps the data came from a single study that was poorly performed and then cited in everyone else's literature. But after exhaustive digging, that didn't seem to be the case. Everyone's tests of mouse telomeres in the field came to the same conclusion. It was simply considered a fact that mice had unusually long telomeres.

This unexpected roadblock to what seemed like a slam-dunk hypothesis bothered Weinstein for weeks. Finally, after enough contemplation, he began to wonder if the fact that mice have extraordinarily long telomeres wasn't a trait that was typical to mice in general. What if it were a trait of the specific mice that were being tested by scientists?

To his surprise, when Bret looked into this possibility, it turned out that nearly all of the model laboratory mice that were used in scientific studies were the same species — called *Mus Musculus*. But what *really* shocked him was when his digging discovered that nearly *all* of the Mus Musculus in America came from a *single* lab in the eastern coastal state of Maine!

Could it be that mice themselves don't simply have enormously long telomeres naturally? Is it instead the case that scientists simply thought this because they were all testing from the very same genetic pool of laboratory stock?

This (if it were true) could not only change the way that geneticists saw mouse telomeres, antagonistic pleiotropies, and senescence in general; the possibilities this hypothesis suggested could have radically dangerous implications in the medical sciences who relied so heavily on these animals in their testing.

Think of it like this: what a mouse with extraordinarily long telomeres gets for their effect is a preternatural ability to heal itself at the cellular level. While, in exchange for this super healing ability early in life, they would almost certainly all die from cancer later in life. Since their cells all have unbelievably large Hayflick limits.

How that may play out in pharmaceutical testing could lead researchers to pass drugs that don't seem to have any concerning degree of toxicity in their lab mice (because of their unnatural ability to resist toxic damage). When, at a human level, the same drug that seemed fine in Mus Musculus could accumulate cellular damage in humans once it reached the market. And that could lead to death from a drug that seemed otherwise safe in their safety trials.

Remember earlier when we were looking into the Thalidomide trials? They only tested the drug on mice, and *only* for toxic effects on them. Though it would be impossible to trace the genetic ancestors of lab mice back to the 1950s to confirm or deny their telomere lengths, there are even more recent drugs that this may also be a contributing factor to concerning their disasters in human use.

You may be objecting that toxic traits in pharmaceutical trials (even if they were invisible at the animal testing phase, called phase two) would become evident in the human testing phase of the trials (called phase three). But that would only be the case if the damages were acute (happen in the short term). One of a number of weak points in human cellular biology when it comes to their ability to repair themselves is found in heart cells. When damaged, they tend to repair using scar tissue instead of more heart cells. This is thought to be a natural attempt to prevent the possibility of cancers in the heart. Any degree of abnormality in the structure of the heart muscles presents a higher likelihood of causing arrhythmias or infarctions. But if a pharmaceutical that caused cellular toxicity across the entire body didn't kill those super-mice in phase two, it may cause enough systemic damage in humans to accrue in the heart tissues of those people in phase three. People with cardiac damage may not have direct cardiac failure for many months or years after the fact. And, by that point, the drug has already been approved and released to the public en masse.

This is the story of the drug Vioxx, released by Merck in 1999. By the time it was pulled from the market in 2004, the stories of heart attacks and strokes from its users were becoming a societal nightmare. By 2007, Merck wound up settling to the tune of $5 billion (one of the largest lawsuits in pharmaceutical history). The number of total lives lost in the time this drug was on the market is estimated anywhere between 50,000 to 500,000 world wide.

Would the safety signals have shown up in animal trials if the model animals weren't abnormally resistant to cellular damage? No one can know at this point. But the story of these mice and this discovery that Weinstein made doesn't stop there.

After he had discovered the connection between lab mice, their lineage, and the solitary lab they were being bred and distributed from, Bret (a graduate student by now) would reach out to a famous PhD in this field — Carol Greider — to request that she look into this hypothesis to find out if all mice have this genetic trait, or just these particular Mus Musculus. Little did he know at this point, but the entire structure of the sciences, their representatives, and their attendant academies were in fact a complicated spiderweb of reputational hierarchies and self-serving interests.

Greider would have one of her graduate students run the tests that Weinstein suggested they run. He would in turn, soon respond through email saying Bret's intuitions were correct! Once inter-species comparisons were completed between other mice and those lab grown lines the difference in telomere length was stark. Bret was over-the-moon when he heard this conclusion! The next obvious step at this point was to send their findings to a journal to be presented for peer review. He would reach out to Carol asking where she planned to publish *her* paper on the test they had run so he could cite it in the paper *he* planned on writing. Oddly, the response he got back from her was that she wasn't going to write any paper and instead planned on simply keeping the information "in-house".

Though confused by her response, Weinstein would write up his paper, complete with the entire hypothesis, testing, and citations. But (for lack of any citation from Greider) before sending it out to a journal, he decided to send it to George Williams — the world's most eminent scientist on senescence and the man who wrote the paper on antagonistic pleiotropy. Williams gave a beaming review of the work and sent it back with his personal recommendation that any journal take this work *extremely* seriously. At that point, Weinstein sent it away to the journal *Nature*.

To his utter confusion, the paper would be sent back as rejected without review. It was beyond disheartening, it was tantamount to impossible, being that it came with the personal recommendation of the world's leading researcher in the field.

While still reeling after the rejection letter from *Nature*, Bret would be contacted out of the blue by a much smaller and obscure journal called *Experimental Gerontology*. They stated that they had heard rumor of his paper and would like for him to send it to them for review. Being that Bret had never reached out to them before, it's likely that George Williams had heard of *Nature*'s rejection of the paper and then reached out to his network of friends to find somewhere else to have it published. This is pertinent to note to reveal the degree to which those in authority within the sciences hold the power to sway their establishment. And that realization isn't only relevant to this part of the story.

He would indeed send his paper away for review to *Experimental Gerontology*. It's important to state that the review process before publishing is done *blind*. This means that whoever the reviewer is is not made known to the authors. And although this is the case, it is realistically quite obvious who does the reviewing based upon their style. And even more so in smaller fields of research like that of cellular senescence.

The review would be sent back to Weinstein. When it was, two things were obvious. One, that the reviewer was almost certainly Carol Greider. And two, that she was attempting to make it look utterly riddled with flaws. But, beyond those two observations, another glaring pattern was that the plethora of flaws being proposed by this reviewer were all bogus. It was clear that they wanted the paper killed and rejected.

If he was beginning to become suspicious of Greider's intentions regarding this research before, now it was becoming much more clear. If this information were to become public knowledge among the sciences, that mouse telomeres weren't naturally long, every laboratory studying senescence around the world would have access to this valuable knowledge. But, you may ask, isn't that what you would want for science to work? Isn't that how human progression from the effort of communal aggregation of discoveries builds forward into the future?

Take this query out of the realm of the theoretical scientific process and, instead, answer it from a realistic, human perspective. Greider was deep into her career when she had this breakthrough discovery fall into her lap. She was already well on her way to a Nobel prize some day with the research she had done in her field. But if she could not only have this valuable knowledge first but also make sure that her lab was the *only* one who had it; to any outside observer who didn't know what she knew, every hypothesis that used this information to effect would appear like she had a super genius level of prediction. This would bolster her legacy nearing the end of her career and all but guarantee her a Nobel prize or two.

This seems like the only reason that someone in her position would opt to keep such extraordinary knowledge "in-house".

In the mean time, every single drug trial that relied on these model animals to predict health outcomes in humans would remain skewed at best and mortally flawed at worst. The human cost of not bringing this information to the forefront cannot be understated. Beyond the material damage and loss of life, the ethereal effects upon the sciences were knowingly continued for the sake of one person's self-interest. That is to say, every laboratory test that used these animals as empirical proof flawed the accepted science of the day.

Both before this discovery but, most importantly, after it as well.

Weinstein's paper that was submitted to *Experimental Gerontology* would wind up being approved and published, regardless of the reviewer's dismissal of it, but it didn't appear to make any waves.

Carol Greider would go on to win a Nobel Prize in 2009 for her earlier discovery of the enzyme telomerase, which is responsible for shortening chromosomal telomeres.

As of 2020, Weinstein stated that he was unaware of whether or not the industry had corrected the problem with Mus Musculus model lines. Being that so many scientific papers, reputations, and tests would be negatively affected if not invalidated by such a bombshell — not to mention the destruction of a mechanism within the pharmaceutical industry that allowed them to get products to market more often — I'll leave it with the reader to intuit if this correction is likely to have happened or not.

LOGIC AND RATIONALISM

We began our look into Truth in science with the *empirical* for the simple reason that it relates almost entirely to the layer of reality that we exist in. The layer of physical reality. And although this is the most obvious and actionable layer for us to focus upon, it's by no means the only layer there is. And, perhaps, not even the most important layer of them all. Though, granted, that's a foreign thought for those of us who primarily track our reality within it.

When I introduced the idea of the three pillars earlier, I presented another model of them where they blend from one to the next along a spectrum. Starting with the scientific on one end and the theologic on the other and connected by the mediating third pillar of philosophy. As we start meandering away from the rigid practice of the empirically scientific, this pillar will begin to blend more into the next along that spectrum.

The most popular and contrasting scientific methodology to empiricism is that of rationalism. And in this portion of the scientific pillar, more of what will be found in the philosophic ahead is added to the scientific, which presents extrinsic avenues that permit a further expansion outside of the circle of empirical orthodoxy.

Rationalism doesn't hold the human senses as highly as it does man's control of logic and reason to define the unknown around him. And although this fearlessly and unapologetically wades outside of the empirically tangible, some of its constituents are regarded as perhaps the truest layers within science as a whole.

Chief among these is mathematics. Famous astronomer Galileo Galilei once said, *"Mathematics is the language in which God has written the universe."*. The physical layer of reality is quantifiable. This has been a reliable rock on which all of the scientific has been built upon. (Interestingly, this itself is an *a priori* that comes from the theological end of the spectrum. We'll come back to that later in the book.) The quantization of the physical is made possible and reliable by the existence of logic within the system. This allows the use of logic and reason to accurately divine what is true, not only within the material layer of reality but (to some extent) the ethereal as well.

For those of us who were taught that mathematics was a "hard science", the proof of such was explicitly obvious. 1 + 1 = 2 every time. And the material application of this can be seen as true by a toddler. It may be surprising, then, to find that such a rudimentary and applicable aspect of science is placed most suitably within a methodology that blends into the philosophical and farther from the empirical. This blending, in fact, is quite obvious — you can rationally state that 2 x 2 = 4 without having to group two sets of two physical things to prove it — but what's less obvious is the ability that mathematicians have to delaminate them. This is sometimes delineated by the terminological difference between arithmetic and mathematics. You could equate their difference to that of letters and language. The former represents the substrate of the latter, but the latter is not derivative in meaning from the former. Words and the stories they tell are an affectation of the artist who wields them. The letters, on their own, don't imbue the artist's meaning without his intent. This was shown in my previous book, *Consciousness Reality & Purpose*, when philosopher John Searl resolved the difference between an intelligent computer and a conscious person in a thought experiment called the Chinese Room. Searl made it clear that the difference between the two is *intentionality*. And in the same way, the realm of mathematics can be used (as a poet uses a language) to imbue the intentionality of a mathematician's hypothetical intention. This, though, can lead the hard science of math into the theoretical realm of educated supposition.

Rationalism is almost exclusively contained within the ethereal. What makes it powerful is the degree to which it can be transposed accurately upon the layer of the material after the fact. You can rationalize material properties in the ethereal (namely, within your mind), then layer them back upon the material as a way to test its accuracy. You may wonder what the difference is between this and straight-up empiricism. The immediate answer would be the difference between starting with an observation and starting with an intuition. There are two other answers to it, though, that can be seen from both the philosophic and the scientific bents. Philosophically (and we will dive much more deeply into this aspect in the next chapter), you can rationalize the effects of an immaterial system — take political systems for instance — in a way that empiricism cannot. While scientifically, entirely immaterial, theoretical constructs can be layered upon each other in ways that rarely, if ever, require any transposition back onto the material at all.

This is both the power and the problem of theoretical mathematics and rationalism as a whole. Being able to use a form of scientific exercise to endeavor outside the realm of the empirically provable opens up avenues that would otherwise remain inaccessible to us from the material layer. Simultaneously, though, by stretching our reach further and further from the firm ground of the material, we become more vulnerable to creating false realities that appear to be reinforced by mathematical rigor.

The more rationalistic hypotheses that get stacked one on top of another, the more likely they are to diverge at any given point from what is true. Especially if they aren't being required to be qualified in the material along the way. Now, that doesn't mean that great work that leads to empirical proofs many years after their inception hasn't happened. In fact, part of Einstein's theory of general relativity predicted an astronomical effect called gravitational waves nearly 100 years before it was proven empirically. The problem was, within those 100 years, that any other hypotheses that built atop of the gravitational waves theory did so on the presupposition that general relativity was correct. And that may seem like a non-issue past the point where we know it's been witnessed materially, but 100 years is a long time to be hoping that the best theory is correct before you know it is. And just like the mouse telomere story above, if it were found to be incorrect, would science amend not only that theory but all of the hypotheses built upon it over the span of the last century?

The answer to that question is going to necessarily have to take into account the likely corruption of Moloch in the system. Whether that delays the correction of rationalistic science or prevents it altogether is something that's difficult to know for certain or as some de facto property of the process. The best we can do in the present is to track how these instances have played out historically up until this point. And there's much to be said about that. Historically, it would appear that, given enough time (sometimes in the order of centuries), scientific progression continues regardless of peoples or powers trying to prevent it. But to then take that as a reliable principal may be misguided for a couple of reasons.

Firstly, although humanity sociologically doesn't change very much over time — our base and higher natures remain essentially consistent — the specific people and power structures of any given point of time are unique. This presents a variable that may effect both the likelihood and the direction of balancing based upon their interaction with the dilemma.

Secondly, the direction that gets decided upon will make all the difference. And it's not a binary proposition. You may think, in a two-dimensional manner, that science will either correct or it won't. But, in a more three dimensional manner, any correction simply presents a new trajectory — not necessarily a true one.

If we can recognize that what we think is science may need to be corrected, the correction we make isn't necessarily true by default. All we had identified was a falsehood. That doesn't present what's true as the only other alternative.

This is the precarious dance that we communally make as humanity endeavors to forward its understanding of the unknown beyond what we can corporeally qualify. Recognizing all along the way that what we are doing is grasping in the dark to try and build the most usable version of limited reality that we can for our purposes. And those efforts, by nature, are bound to be constructs within the whole, while not the whole itself.

A CONSTRUCT OF LAYERS

In the 1970s, physicist Thomas Kuhn published a book that has become a standard barer within the sciences when it comes to the philosophical understanding of how and why science changes over time in what appears less like a progression and more like various revolutions.

In the book *The Structure of Scientific Revolutions*, Kuhn presented a concept that was new to the philosophy of science at the time. It was a concept he coined as "paradigms". Today, when you use the word paradigm when describing a way of viewing something, everyone understands what you mean when you say that. But back when this book was published, this was a novel consideration that was effectively heterodox to the norm.

What this concept described, if transposed into the construct I've laid out in the introduction, would be an entire ontological tree of scientific understanding. I called these "constructs". Something that started from either an a priori or datum point, that then branched out from there into the unknown, describing what it found as it related to the previous discoveries in that process, all the way back to the starting point.

With this understanding of what Kuhn meant when he said "paradigm", or what I mean when I say "construct", the related concept of "paradigm shifts" explain why science can more accurately be seen as a series of revolutions than a steady and linear progression over time. When a paradigm shift occurs, the existing orthodoxy within a science may get taken backwards down the ontological tree all the way down to the root presumption in what is referred to as "first principles" thinking.

To question an entire orthodoxological paradigm down to its root proposition is quite an affront to any field of scientific inquiry. And this is why, when such questioning eventually gets born out as appropriate, the best description of what proceeds is a revolution. And revolutions must be fought, they don't just quietly happen. All of the explicit examples given earlier in this chapter can attest to that.

Kuhn would conclude that this is the actual, messy reality of how science progresses over time. I would agree, but I would also like to go a few steps further within the meta conversation itself as well as the resolution of my own construct proposed in the introduction; that of layers of Truth. Starting with pulling back the lens on paradigms or constructs to view them as a whole.

If you were to picture, in your mind's eye, an entire construct — a widely branching tree of nodes that have a starting point but no definite end in any direction forward, floating in an infinite black abyss of the unknown — this is how I picture any particular paradigm. Past or present. All of them are a communal but proprietary effort to track things that are true based upon some starting presumption. Picturing them as such brings into stark focus how precarious the entire endeavor is as a whole. So many paradigms have begun, been expanded upon, and collapsed in the wake of a repeating pattern of scientific revolutions. To believe that the present constructs we exist within are better than those of the past is one thing, but to presume that they are Truth is (logically and historically) folly.

Accepting this can feel like a step towards nihilism. What is the point of trying in that case? But this too is folly. Even besides the obvious and tangible technological advances made by way of scientific revolutions, the acceptance that we almost certainly don't know the Truth of a given layer should serve as both a vital dose of humility and an actionable infusion of inspiration to continue the search.

And now, to speak to layers themselves, how do they fit within the concept of emmet as opposed to what we build throughout the two with our proprietary ontological constructs? Like so many things in this reality, I see it as a fractal reflection of reality itself projected from us back upon it.

What total reality is consists of every layer of it that we know (as well as every layer that we don't) unified together in an interconnection of them all that relies upon the whole network, but to varying degrees at any given point within it. How those points vary by degrees relates to the connection or separation of layers within the total network itself.

In a similar way to how a complete human brain has a myriad of interconnected neurons connected by a cobweb of specific synapses, layers (and their entire Truth fragments within them) connect to other layers through true things that exist in both; thus creating the entirety of the total Truth.

The fractal nature of this construct is seen at the level of our own efforts to build proprietary constructs from (primarily) subsets within layers. In our attempt to transmute the unknown into categories of known, we create a lattice work of subsets within differing layers that connect to each other through true things that exist in each. If a bubble (a subset) is created within a layer, a line between a true thing that exists in a different layer can be drawn to another subset in the second layer based on their similarity. This is typically how we build out our ontological constructs within all the layers that we can access.

At the level of each individual subset, work can continue to be done to expand the bubble outward within the layer it exists in. In that process, more connections may be sent out as new true things are added to the subset from the remainder of the Truth fragment it exists in to other subsets that share that true thing within another layer.

The issue that then arises at some point within this effort that precipitates a revolution of the construct in part or in whole is that there are always missing pieces within each layer that the subset doesn't yet know. Between the (often) unintentional omission of these true things and the compounding of them over the number of subsets used to build out a construct, those fractal and incomplete structures stop mapping so eloquently over top of emmet in their application.

In my personal opinion, it's modern science's myopic and even arrogant view of itself in this dynamic that has led so many brilliant people within it to minimize, relegate, and even obfuscate as irrelevant the other two pillars of philosophic and theologic exploration and discovery. Based on where we most tangibly sit in total reality, many of these people consider the entirety of it must be within our reach and then further constrain this reach within the sciences. When it's not only possible but likely that total Truth and the total reality it pertains to stretches widely outside of our reach while, at the same time, effects (either directly or indirectly) those layers we're most comfortable describing.

In the visible and relevant ways that science itself has stumbled and collapsed by ignoring or conflating layers of Truth in its own constructs — for example between mice and men or between laboratory and society — a prudent pause and reflection upon what is and what can be known should be a constant feature of this pillar. This is something that the next pillar is incredibly well suited for. Which is why their union is not only natural, but is ignored at our intellectual and physical peril.

Thus (to come back to the beginning of this chapter) what I've written may seem overly harsh or incisive of science, but I intend these criticisms to be solely focused upon the dangerous tendency man has to use it as a zero-sum solution.

The scientific process is a beautiful, functional, and elegant tool of sensemaking that has served us well while attempting to parse the known from the unknown. But it's through the religious fervor of those scientific zealots, who would limit the scope of total Truth within the processes they have self-defined, that we wind up profaning the very sanctum of science in so doing.

In the next chapter, we will blend from the scientific into the philosophic. In this effort we'll explore the union they create, the differences in application that philosophy offers, and the final blending that logically follows from this vital mediating pillar.

CHAPTER III

TRUTH IN PHILOSOPHY

"The mind of man is capable of anything — because everything is in it, all the past as well as all the future. What was there after all?

Joy, fear, sorrow, devotion, valor, rage — who can tell? — but truth — truth stripped of its cloak of time."

— JOSEPH CONRAD

3

TRUTH IN PHILOSOPHY

"We do not receive wisdom; we must discover it for ourselves after a journey that no one can take for us or spare us."

— MARCEL PROUST

What, effectively, is the difference between knowledge and wisdom? Some may not even realize there exists a difference to speak of. They may say, "Wisdom can't be had without knowledge; therefore wisdom, is knowledge accumulated and used to affect.". And though this isn't strictly wrong, there is a significant difference that still exists. One that, if overlooked, is the very definition of unwise.

You can have knowledge without wisdom, and wisdom without specific knowledge. What differentiates strict knowledge from wisdom is the ability to discern what is true. It's this discernment that comes, not from a book or a lecture, but from experience in the practice of all three pillars — scientific, philosophic and theologic.

The very word *Philosophy* comes from the Latin word *Philosophia*. Its two root words are *Phílos*, meaning loving, and *Sophía*, meaning wisdom. Thus philosophy is the love of wisdom.

It may seem strange then that, in the historical application and exploration of philosophy, many different and even contradictory schools of thought have arisen. How is it that wisdom can be applied to the same questions and produce differing answers? That would seem antithetical to the idea of objective Truth itself!

In this chapter's focus, we will dive into the history and etymology of several popular philosophical views of reality. Their material uses, their stalwarts, and the layers that open up through their unique constructs of creation.

Wisdom, as it turns out, is less of a noun and more of a verb. And without a persistent effort — a love — to stay true to its guidance, man can float adrift without an anchor into the fathomless oceans of ethereal thought.

In the preparation of writing my previous book, where I first presented the idea of the three pillars, I asked myself what the most defining quality of the theologic was. What was it that set it apart from the scientific and the philosophic in effect? The answer to that question, I found, came from asking what its opposite pillar — science — held most highly. It was simple for me to qualify that, and when I did, the first question's answer became very clear.

If the highest regarded quality of science is proof, then the highest regarded quality of theology is its diametric opposite — faith.

Philosophy, in this regard, finds itself quite comfortably between those two extremes. Science regards faith as folly and theology regards proof as superfluous. This is why philosophy not only connects the two together as a mediating center, but is found prominently in both.

Science cannot rationalize qualitative data without a philosophy of the system it stems from. Science in itself has a dedicated field of philosophic study called *Philosophy of Science*, where the very nature of the scientific process and each of its functional mechanics are rationally observed and considered apart from their practical applications.

Theology also has deep philosophic foundations as a necessary intermediary between experiential spirituality and the logical frameworks we house them within for the sake of cognitive intelligibility.

Philosophy's multivariate uses situate it in a vital and eminent position where, through the effort of thoughtful introspection and an honest search for Truth, wisdom serves as a divining rod to lead men through an endless maze of possibility.

PHILOSOPHIC RATIONALITY

One of the enduring qualities that an aspiring philosopher is encouraged by their forebears to cultivate is to understand understanding. To seek out not *what* to learn, but *how* to learn.

Therefore, the first task of the philosophical is to define the difference between those two things and nurture the mindset that makes that definition obvious. This, in its own right, is a form of rationalism. But it is not a rationalism that is as tangible as what is seen in the sciences. It's a form of meta-heuristic that underlies any honest search for Truth in all fields.

When any conversation around the philosophical arises, it's difficult not to start with or come back to the renowned philosophers of ancient Greece. Though there is much that can be said about older philosophical schools from other and disparate traditions (and we will come to some of those later in this chapter), the majority of western culture owes its roots to these thoughts and the progenitors who forwarded them.

Chief among them, chronologically, was Socrates. For a man who is so universally revered for his thoughts, Socrates never actually wrote any of them down. It was his later student, Plato, who chronicled his tutor's methods and conversations for posterity.

Instead of writing his thoughts and theories down, Socrates preferred to dialogue with people in person. He considered written thoughts as "dead" thoughts. They have no life because they cannot change or be challenged in real time. His particular method of dialogue was so unique in his time that it was named after him as its own mode of conversation, called the Socratic Method or Socratic Dialogue.

The defining feature of the Socratic Method of conversation is a form of questioning from one party to the other that requires *them* to answer, instead of simply producing your own answer for them. In this way, it cultivates the ability to learn *how* to think, not just *what* to think. Moreover, the party who's required to form an answer will have to justify to themselves and the other party why they came to that answer. Further leading them to reflect upon their own beliefs and thought processes.

For example, one might say, "Our society is run by democratic rule. Why do you think that is?" The other party in the dialogue would form their response, and then be met with, "Do you think it's the correct method for our society?" Then, (if it wasn't explicit in this response), they would be asked to explain why they think that.

Some people see this form of conversation as adversarial, but the purpose of its method is to require only well-considered responses while rooting out any beliefs that have no foundation beneath them. In so doing, both the person answering and the person questioning gain from the interaction. Either the respondent finds a flaw in their own thoughts or the questioner learns from their well-formed opinions.

It was this particular style of dialogue that was not only furthered by Plato after Socrates died, but also used in a novel way to memorialize his beloved mentor. In fact, scholars believe it was the death of Socrates — one that involved political entrapment and eventual suicide by poison — that drove Plato to begin his many writings that now make up so much of our understanding of philosophy in the west.

Plato ingeniously melded together the Socratic method of dialogue with the most popular form of storytelling at that time in Athens — theater. Typically, books of that time and the times that preceded it were written in a form called a treatise. A treatise is, in effect, the author writing *at* the reader. Whereas a dialogue was a conversation between multiple parties in the writing. This modality allowed Plato to both ride upon the popularity of Athenian theatrical storytelling while posthumously carrying on the legacy of Socrates through Socratic conversations between the story's characters.

Through the works of over two dozen Platonic dialogues, Plato explored everything from material systems to social constructs, emotional dynamics to personality traits. If Socrates was the revolutionary of western philosophy, Plato was the prolific writer who allowed for his revolution to carry on thousands of years into the future. But any exploration into the ancient Grecian philosophers wouldn't be complete without speaking to a contemporary of Plato's and a man so well regarded in this space that later theological philosopher Thomas Aquinas would simply call him 'The Philosopher' —Aristotle.

Polymath, personal tutor to Alexander the Great and the man largely responsible for the future methodological scientific systems of the west, Aristotle's contributions to our current understanding of philosophy cannot be overstated. He would champion and deeply resolve the ideas of human virtues. Their ideal expressions as well as their vices of deficiency and excess. In his work *Nicomachean Ethics*, Aristotle laid out in detail twelve human virtues he considered worthy of aspiration. They were: courage, temperance, liberality, magnificence, magnanimity, ambition, patience, friendliness, truthfulness, wit, modesty, and justice. He considered the acquisition of these virtues in one's life akin to achieving happiness.

On either side of each virtue he placed a related trait that; on one side, would be the result of not enough of the virtue and on the other side, too much. For example, of truthfulness he would say the the vice of deficiency was self-deprecation; while on the other side, the vice of excess was boastfulness. The goal by Aristotle's estimation was to endeavor, in all virtues, to find the perfect balance between each vice. This he called the "golden mean".

He also birthed a particular form of speaking that is used to this day by orators, politicians, and teachers called rhetoric. Rhetorical speaking is formed in away that's meant to engage and convince an audience to supporting the ideas of the rhetorician. By using humor, analogy, and an understanding of the emotional impact of a subject, a skilled rhetorician can bring any crowd around to their side of a debate regardless of the Truth of the matter.

Rhetoric is such a powerful form of intellectual magic that it can be used to bring an ignorant crowd to enlightenment or an enlightened crowd into ignorance. It's a philosophical tool that was used effectively by Martin Luther King Jr. and Adolf Hitler alike.

This is an incredibly important point to recognize about philosophy. The exploration for wisdom doesn't necessitate the use of what it affords its explorer to be good or true. Wisdom can be both discovered and subsequently branched away from in a manner that's sometimes hard to notice. Knowing how to manipulate people may take an appreciable amount of wisdom regarding the systems that govern them. But does that require those who understand these things to act wisely? This is where many of the philosophers above and many who proceeded them strained heavily to instill an onus of morality into their questions.

Using the methodological framework of philosophy can produce incredible advances in theory and technology. But the implementation of those products of wisdom can further be used and abused in the most unwise ways. It was for this reason that philosophers constantly wrestled with the idea of morals and ethics as a form of stop-gate against abuses that wisdom can afford those who understand its power.

If (returning to our analogy of the spectrum) the scientific blends at its leading edge into the philosophical by way of rationalism, then as we move further into the more purely philosophical pillar, we begin to see its ideal uses within humanity that the scientific pillar simply cannot adequately be used for.

WHAT IS AND WHAT OUGHT

We started this chapter with the observation that there is a difference between knowledge and wisdom. That difference has to do with being able to discern what is true. And this happens every time you try to qualify what is true about an objective thing. But what if the question you need to use wisdom to answer isn't objective? What if it's subjective? More to the point, what does philosophy do with questions of morality if morality isn't already defined?

Ethics and morals are subjects that have deeply concerned philosophers for a very long time. And part of the reason for that concern doesn't even relate to the use or abuse of objective wisdom, but rather to the question of how to even define what is or isn't moral.

Remember how we talked about those scientific revolutions that could topple an entire instantiated paradigm all the way back to its a priori datum point? Philosophers have, since time immemorial, come back to a question of first principles — a questioning of man's foundational presuppositions — in regards to what a person *ought* to do. Moral obligations. Ethical concerns.

What *is* wise as a fundamental ethos of humanity.

This is a vital layer of emmet that the processes of science may prove maladapeted to the field. Yet for lack of consideration, can, have, and do intersect with science in ways that have lead to catastrophes like those mentioned in chapter one.

The Greek philosophers above and their later intellectual decedents, the Stoics, spoke heavily to the idea of virtues. What are the virtuous things a person should aspire to cultivate in themselves? And what are their mirror opposites? The deeper layer question that preempts this line of reasoning was something these thinkers also weighed in upon — are these virtues objective or subjective?

Socrates, Plato, and Aristotle all spoke in some manner to ideas of "form" or "substance". Later these thoughts would be re-categorized by people like Thomas Aquinas as "transcendentals". Something that is transcendental is, by definition, a priori true or correct, regardless of subjectivity. Aquinas would further sub-categorize the idea of transcendentals into six columns: *ens, res, unum, aliquid, bonum, verum* — or *being, thing, one, something, good, and true*. Furthermore, he would unify these back into a single transcendental quality by stating that something from each category naturally begets the others. For example, if something is good it is also true.

Transcendentality as both a concept and a starting point makes the effort to discover and qualify the Truth a very derivative proposition. There's a standard to compare thoughts, statements, and situations against. But as time would continue and later philosophers would continue in their exploration into morality and ethics, the question persisted. Were there actually transcendental Truths? And if so, are we even capable of deciphering them from our limited perspectives?

And it really does come down to a question of perspective from our position.

An entire genre within philosophy called ethical dilemmas deeply obscures the idea of transcendental moral imperatives. If you're stuck between a rock and a hard place, is the lesser of two evils always correct? Can something seen as an objective evil be a subjective good? In that case, what is transcendentally true?

One of the most common ethical dilemmas philosophy and psychology students are presented with is some form of what is referred to as a *Trolley Problem*. It sets the stage as such:

You stand at the switch of a train track that allows you to choose which of two tracks a speeding trolley will take. On one side, six people are tied up laying across the tracks and will surely all die if the trolley goes down that path. On the other side, one person is tied up and will surely die if the trolley goes down that path. Which do you choose?

Logic would dictate that the side with one person is the more ethically correct track to select. But what if that person was going to discover the cure for cancer if they survived? If you knew that information, would it change your decision?

If you didn't know that information, yet it was true, would that change what was the correct choice?

What if the one person tied up was your own child? Or even worse, what if it was the man who *killed* your child? What is the ethically correct decision then? Do transcendental virtues account for subjective morality?

There seems to be a splitting of layers in these questions. Where what is objectively true can simultaneously be subjectively wrong. If there is an emmet of total Truth, one out of two answers must be true, right? Well yes, but actually no. Because both options would be true, though only within the layer of their consideration.

But how are we, who can only act subjectively, supposed to discern what is more moral or ethical if both answers make their case depending on the perspective you ask them from?

A more modern and continually debated ethical dilemma that acutely resolves the level and existential weight of these fundamental questions happened on August 6th and August 9th, 1945. After six years of the worst world war in human history, the United States dropped two atomic bombs on the Japanese civilian populations of Hiroshima and Nagasaki. The resulting causalities would be estimated at around a quarter of a million people dead. Though, by these actions the final end of World War II — a war that claimed the lives of some 70-85 million people — would be achieved.

Objectively, the ends would seem to justify the means. But this real life trolley problem gets harder the more you look into the details of it.

On the American side, the atom bomb that was the result of years of secret research

(code named the Manhattan Project) was meant to be used to fight the Nazis on the western front of the war. But by the time it was finally successfully tested, in a historic spectacle called the trinity explosion, Hitler was already dead and Berlin had fallen with the entire Nazi Third-Reich in tow. The only remaining theater of war was the pacific theater where the Americans and other allies were relentlessly beating a failing Japanese imperial army. There was a real debate at the time, even espoused by some of the scientists who were part of the Manhattan Project, about whether they needed to use the atomic bombs anymore. Japan was losing, and the question seemed to be more of a matter of time than a matter of fact.

The argument opposed to this suggestion to spare the bombs revolved around a sort of trolley problem. For every day that Japan didn't surrender, more allied lives were being needlessly lost if, in fact, the bombs would seal the end of the war. Now, here President Harry Truman sat at the throw-switch of the tracks. On one side, a possible quick end to the war and a lessening of American military deaths. On the other side, a likely lengthening of the war leading to the eventual surrender of Japan anyways. The choice would seem clear.

Except, from Truman's position, the dropping of the bombs was never actually a sure end to the war. In fact, up to that point in the war, the eventually accepted tactic of blanket carpet bombing entire civilian cities with incendiary ordnance was common place and would result in the wholesale destruction of up to 100,000 human lives in a single raid. None of those raids were ever effective in causing the surrender of the countries they were inflicted upon. More to the point, Japan *itself* was being fire bombed by the US constantly on the lead up towards the atomic actions and they persistently rejected the allied pleas for their surrender to prevent more of their citizen's deaths. It was stated time and again that the imperial army's credo was akin to a suicide pact. They were not to be defeated by the threat or affect of human deaths, no matter the numbers or implement.

So again, from President Truman's perspective, could his decision to drop the bombs anyway be seen as morally correct? The argument is typically made with the benefit of foresight, but we all exist in the present so do we even have a claim to moral objective Truth from our subjective positions?

The bombs would be dropped. Between 100,000 and 200,000 innocent civilian men, women, and children would die horrifically in Hiroshima and another 70,000 to 100,000 in Nagasaki. From their point of view, was Truman's decision morally correct? How many of them would have survived the war if he hadn't? We can never know those counter-factual numbers. But to give air to the subjective experience of those on the ground at these locations, I'd like to present a first-hand account of a survivor named Asami Okoshi — who only survived by chance because she was inside a cement bathroom that collapsed around her without killing her — as presented in history podcaster Dan Carlin's exposé into the incidents called Destroyer of Worlds:

"Looking around for my sister, I saw her sprawled outside of the corridor. The right side of her body covered in terrible burns. She had probably been washing her hands with her right hand stretched over the wash basin when caught by the searing heat.

I put my sister on my back and fled barefoot to Hijiyama park. Her face was festering from her burns and her right eye was hanging out. I pushed the eye back into its socket and tried to use a gauze mask to hold it into place, but her ear had melted away and there was nothing to attach the mask to.

Her mouth was twisted to the right and she could do no more than whimper for water; only the first syllable of the word emerging distinctly. On reaching Hijiyama park, I laid my sister down on the ground and set off to search for my children.

The fires were still burning fiercely. In a street car that had been burning bright red, surrounded by people who had already been killed by the fire, I saw a woman holding onto a strap and calling for help. The intense heat prevented me from approaching her, however. There was nothing I could do.

To a man sitting on some stone steps I said, 'Come on! Lets get away from here!', and pulled him up by the hand. But as I did so, the skin came away from his hand and he fell slowly to the ground. I could see his shadow imprinted clearly on the wall behind him where he had been sitting.

Many people called out to me for help or water. Unburned because having been in the lavatory, I could only bring my hands together and apologize to the people I passed as I searched for some sign of my children.

As it turned out, none of those who left that morning ever came home again. Not my five children, not my grandfather, my sister Machiko or my cousin. Not a bone remained for me to find and treasure. Our house burned down so that I hadn't even a photograph to remember them by.

My sister Hisako drew her last breath four days later on the evening of August 10th in agony from her massive injuries. I will never forget the expression on her face when I tried to give her a drop of water... I was alone."

Stories of children leaping to their deaths from the third story windows of their school buildings in an attempt to escape raging fires are common place among endless other accounts of unmitigated horror. From those people's perspective, would they agree with the morality of the atomic bombs? If the story above was yours and it was your family vaporized in an instant, would you agree with Truman's actions? If Truman knew what horrors these bombs would cause, would he have dropped them on his *own* family if he knew it would end a war?

The idea of objective, transcendental morality or ethical purity inverts when the same questions are asked from the subjective level. Yet the subjective level is where we all live and have to make our decisions from.

Judging again from the future and looking back on the past, many people consider Truman's actions the correct course of action. Militarily, ethically, and morally. Though others would make the point that the use of the atomic bombs didn't just end the second world war but began the proceeding cold war that reposed the trolley problem; but this time with the entire world at wager. In that respect, was there a course of action that could have been better in August of 1945? We'll never know. And where Truth actually resides in between the many confounding and intersecting layers of reality that lead up to those actions may be forever obscured and unanswerable.

The philosophical pillar's objective is to try and guide our subjective choices with the divining rod of wisdom. But we live in a world that is effected not just by wise moral actions but often by unwise and immoral ones. And in the same sense that what defines science on paper doesn't always well represent science in human practice, what we define as the ideal transcendental moral imperatives seem to change significantly in their application depending upon what layer and intent you seek them from.

It's one of the aforementioned qualities of separating layers of Truth that difference can be found when the same action produces differing results. We can see it clearly within ethical dilemmas that there is a difference in answer between an individual and a group. This illuminates another characteristic that is often seen when comparing layers, be they material or ethereal. Scaling up or down within a single system will flow through a variety of different layers that make them up. And as you scale, what is true at one layer may not only be untrue at another but actually be its opposite in application.

This is never more clearly visible than when considering the dynamics of governmental systems. There have existed many different organizations and hierarchies of communal governance. Some of which have worked better than others. The reasons they have worked may not be obviously to the system's credit in some cases, but instead represent a more ideal construct for the variables it governed. Variables like size of the group, cultural history, the level of technological sophistication, etc. As these kinds of considerations change, either scaling up or scaling down, the utility of any certain system of governance is affected in kind.

To make the point clear, let's start with the smallest form of governance and scale up from there. The lowest one can scale down to is the individual, single person. You are the absolute arbiter of your own actions. Any other person trying to force a choice out of you can only do so through cooperation, coercion, or violence. But in each of those cases, the final decision is in the individual's control — their personal governance. Likewise, for you to affect someone else — they being their own master — the same implements of manipulation must be utilized. What people discover, the more they run into this dynamic, is that cooperation is the better method of long-term benefit than other manipulative controls. And through this route, the dynamic of systematic governance changes as the number of individuals in the system scales up.

The next natural level of scale is a family group. At that level, individual mastery hasn't disappeared but organizes into a familial hierarchy between status, age, and responsibility. You could liken it to a small-scale version of a monarchy. At this level there exists a natural patron, matron, and subjects beneath them. Any strain within that system can be controlled and managed by its hierarchical order.

If we now move forward in scale while simultaneously moving backwards in human history, the next natural level of scale is a tribe. This is a number of family units that combine for reasons of language, locality, heritage, genealogy, and communal utility. There are many more roles in this structure, which increases the possibility of personal slight or incongruence (being that almost every individual is now at least two layers removed from their personal concerns). This presents a dynamic that will become more and more acute as the systems scale up. That is, that an ever-present dance must take place between individual concerns and communal ones. Typically, this is mitigated by the instantiation of a leader; someone who the tribe agrees will serve as the communal arbiter who, by definition, supersedes every individual.

The tribal system worked so well for so long that many evolutionary anthropologists suggest its inherent psychology has been hardwired into our brains ever since. But there have been many more levels of scaling since then that continue to change the the utility of our systems and the systems themselves as a result.

As tribes gained not only in number but in technology, the dynamics of families all helping their tribal families out in a communal fashion was scaled and adjusted as well. With the advent of agriculture, massive amounts of resources were able to be created by a very few individuals. This created a boom in the number of people, but also created the necessity to build towns that would become cities. The basic hierarchy of the tribe could scale up for a single city at this point, but another technological invention would radically adjust the dynamic of the entire system — the advent of currency.

Before, the primary concern of everyone within the community was the production of goods and skills that were freely shared among the tribe. This (as well as cultural bonds and the benefits of communal security) was the main mechanism of cohesion between families. When the groups started becoming cities and it became less likely that family groups within them would know or interact with each other, a much more mechanistic utilitarian cohesion would set in. And as cities began trade between other cities where culture wouldn't scale, a system of commerce became the necessary new cohesive modality.

Once we got to the level of nations, then entire cities would act as the family units in a tribe did, except scaled up by order of magnitude. The recognizable system of monarchical governance typically followed up in the form of either a royalty or deity set at the top to serve as leader. But the layers of difference between a familial unit and a true monarchy or dynasty as so far removed in scale from each other that much more structure is necessary to uphold so many people beneath the dictate of a solitary ruler. This is where a political leap in technology spanned the gap between ruler and peasant with many variations of a delineated centralized authority network. Things like Lords and Magistrates would serve as both the arm of the ruler by proxy as well as a means of communication from the bottom of the network to the top.

Bureaucratically, the network above would seem ideal and natural. In reality, the difference of scale between the bottom and the top is so removed that the needs and wants of the individual (at every level) lead to either corruption, abuse, or malcontent and would always end in internal collapse one way or another. Often times, it would be due to the royalty forgetting that the old rule of cooperation was the best maxim to cause people to agree to your terms. Coercion and violence being the common alternatives. And these would cascade with egregious and malevolent disconcern for those at the bottom of the network. They who were the unfortunate receivers in this incongruity of layers would rightfully breed animus and resentment for their lot.

In a different version of delineated networks, the Greeks would be the first to attempt to add the concerns of the people back into the decision making of their rulers. This they called *democracy*, coming from the Greek word *Dēmokratía*. The root words being *dēmos* (meaning people) and *kratos* (meaning rule).

This idea (that born in Greece and later championed by the Roman Republic) presented a theoretical solution to the issues seen under fully autocratic feudal systems. That issue stems from the unmitigated whims of a nation's royalty. In a democratic system, the people at the bottom elect local representatives to intercede on their behalf regarding national decisions and (in theory) retain the ability to oust them by majority vote if they didn't represent well. Neither of those abilities were available to people within a feudal hierarchy.

This too, at the theoretical level, would seem an elegant and sophisticated solution to amend the perennial flaws that become apparent as group dynamics scale up away from the individuals that constitute them. And yet, even with the efforts of some of the wisest philosophers to construct the best system they could, the issues that arise from decisions made at the top would still inevitably constrain or abuse some proportion of the people at the bottom. Notable French political philosopher Alexis de Tocqueville famously compared democracy to a faux totalitarian system when he called it a "tyranny of the masses.". Stating that though the majority in a democratic system would get their way, as many as 49% within that system would be subject to the exact opposite of what they voted for.

Beyond the mathematical tyranny that democracy inflicts upon a number of its citizens, just as the hierarchies of science were indicted in the previous chapter, we cannot ever forget or underestimate the presence of Moloch in these systems. That ever-present human tendency to race to the bottom for personal gain. In the democratic sense, those who get to positions of power by majority vote tend to do so upon campaign promises that they cannot keep. Nor do they intend to once their position has been secured. What's more, in the modern versions of democratic elections, the fealty an elected official is supposed to have to the constituency of people who elected them is often given instead behind the scenes to corporate beneficiaries for all of the same reasons that Moloch is able to set root into human systems. This, at a localized level, is often called crony capitalism. At the systemic level, it's defined as fascism. That is, a blending of corporations and the state.

One of the most radical reactions to these failings of democratic capitalism, in effect, regresses back to a lower level of systemic governance — that of the communal. In an attempt to fully disperse power from the hands of a wealthy oligopoly, *Communism* reverts back to what humanity had at the tribal level of governance. Where things like ownership or wealth had no place among what was a communal partnership between all those who were part of the commune (thus communism). There, perhaps, is no better example to make than the failure of this modality when implemented upon the wrong layer of human groups. At the level of a tribe or a small commune, this system works historically well. While at the level of massive global superpowers and nation states, it has only ever led to historical human atrocities and societal dehumanization.

The communist ideology was first codified and championed by German-born Jewish philosopher and intellectual Karl Marx in his 1848 work, *The Communist Manifesto*. In the proceeding years, communism would serve as solely an academic endeavor but would gain much prominence among certain intellectual thinkers as a possible counter to the follies of capitalism. Though, it would soon get its first chance to play out in the real world shortly into the 20th century.

By 1917, sixty-nine years and one World War removed from the writing of

Marx's manifesto, the Russian Czarist empire would be overthrown during what is known as the Bolshevik revolution. This was communism's chance to bring to fruition the many intellectual musings of nearly seventy years of philosophical prognostication. And these pronouncements spoke to nothing shy of global utopia! Philosophically, intellectually, and theoretically, communism was believed by its proponents to be the harbinger of peace, equity, and unanimity. In application, nothing could have been further from the Truth.

For the century that followed — between what became the communist dictatorships of men like Joseph Stalin, Mao Zedong, and Pol Pot—an estimate of 100-110 million people were either killed or starved to death through the direct implementation of communism. That accounts for over two-thirds of the people killed by all governments, quasi-governments, and guerrillas between the years 1900 and 1987.

What would appear (at a tribal level) to be a functional, rational, and mutually beneficial solution simply doesn't scale up through all of the layers of difference that come with larger human groups. And every real-world attempt to do so has historically caused everything from a stifling of individual rights all the way up to horrific, broad-scale human atrocities.

In the Aristotelian concept of the golden mean, an argument could be made where at the scale of society that democracy is touted to be the best case solution, perhaps the virtuous center between fascism on one end and communism on the other is the ideal structure. Or, it may simply be the most ideal structure we've created thus far. What seems apparent, from the perspective of layering Truth, is that scale matters.

But, where does that leave our questions about objective or transcendental moral Truth? Do they too change as societal scale changes, or are they transcendentally preeminent regardless of scale?

In 1739 Scottish philosopher David Hume, in his paper *A Treatise of Human Nature,* raised a philosophical concern that has persisted in the conversation of morality and ethics ever since. It was a fallacy of conflation that Hume noticed in a philosophical argument between something that "is" and something that "ought". Where defining something that *is* amounts to an objectively descriptive statement; while defining something that *ought* amounts to a subjectively prescriptive statement.

Philosophers utilize this distinctive paradigm in what they call " Hume's Law" or "Hume's Guillotine". The essence of the philosophical law is that you cannot get an *ought* statement from an *is*. Being that the character of *ought* statements are prescriptive, they are either prescribed by the individual (making them subjective) or they're accepted as normative from an external construct of Truth (making them a matter of faith). According to this principle, nothing that objectively *is* carries intrinsic morality or ethical obligation.

Hume's Law utterly distinguishes moral Truth as a subjective enterprise. This position has been lauded by theologians, disputed by scientists, and considered the Achilles heel of society by philosophers over the proceeding years.

Theologically, morality (being detached from the natural world of what *is*) becomes the domain of the transcendental. Many Abrahamic scholars consider that the only reason humanity has morals at all speaks to the Truth of God. Because if the world of man were truly without God, why would any moral imperatives exist in the first place? They contend that without the transcendental moral laws of God first, society would never have looked like it does now; being that what *is* doesn't beget what *ought*. In this way, *is* must not only be subordinate to *ought* but *ought* must have preempted *is* chronologically. Essentially, whatever *ought* to be is good; and God is good. And since God existed before the universe, *ought* predated *is* before man ever came onto the scene. As such, they conclude, morality was an affect of a moral God bestowed upon his creation of what *is*.

The pillar of science brings its own contentions into this dilemma though, in prototypical fashion. Being that the concept of ethics is central to philosophy, and philosophy (in our construct) is centrally between science and theology, both sides of this spectrum bring their particular perspectives to bare on the topic.

In the scientific sense, morality is widely considered by evolutionary psychologists to be a positive adaptation to any social creature. They see no reason why what *ought* shouldn't naturally follow what *is* in the societal sense. Humans (as a creature) are social and thus build societies. That makes human societies themselves an objective *is*. The dynamics of living in a society presuppose predictably adaptive behaviors as to benefit within the society and not to be killed or ostracized by it. Morals, they would contend, have more to do with self preservation and self interest than they do with anything transcendental or divine.

Being that this debate tends to be had in the arena of the philosophical, *that* pillar has presented a possibility that stands apart from both of the others. One philosopher in particular came onto the scene in the latter half of the 19th century that would not only throw a historic wrench into the cog-works of the theological's claim to moral Truth but, in a strange way, into the scientific's as well.

THE MAN WHO MURDERED GOD

Within the many and varied schools of philosophical thought, one of the more modern schools is known as existentialism. Existentialists, perhaps more so than any other branch, focus heavily on the darker and nihilistic (some would say realistic) aspects of what it is to be alive.

If there is beauty and nobility to life, then there must also be the ugly and ignoble parts of living to balance it in return. Between the numerous and horrific examples that history affords us, existence itself can be seen to be as much a curse as it is a blessing.

One of the most utilitarian functions of the theological pillar is its ability to stave off nihilism through faith in an unperceived, transcendental arbiter. Something that can square what appears to so many people to be an unrelenting circular path of suffering and heartbreaking pain.

This type of belief can assuage, perhaps even rationalize, the most atrocious acts of man. But what if the spectrum of our three pillars were to be severed between philosophy and theology?

One man, more than maybe any other in history, lent credence to that cleaving. And by dint of brutal criticism levied against religion, and the structure that upheld it in western culture, he carved the path for that very experiment to be run in earnest for the next one hundred years after his death. On October 15th, 1844, a son was born to Prussian parents in the province of Saxony. His mother was the daughter of a pastor and his father was a pastor himself. To say that young Friedrich Wilhelm Nietzsche grew up in a religious home would be an understatement.

By the time Friedrich was five years old, and in a period of only six months, his father (hardly 35 years old at the time) would die of a terrible brain disease and his two year old brother would also tragically pass. Tragedy, it would seem, would haunt Nietzsche throughout the entirety of his own short and turbulent life.

But in that time, he would produce some of the most paradigm shifting and societal shaking indictments upon God and his followers that modern man, up to that point, had ever witnessed within the western tradition.

The cleaving of theology from philosophy rings of both the logic and spite of a natural genius scorned by existence. This first part of his story must be recognized though because he was, by all accounts, a certifiable genius. The first avenue he would focus his intelligence upon was a fervent and dedicated study of Christian theology.

At the young age of ten, Nietzsche would be accepted to a private school, by way of government scholarship. He focused heavily on religion, European history and language; learning how to read and understand many primary sources in their native tongues. By age twenty, he would move on to the University of Bonn where he continued in the study of theology and classic philology. But, after only a single semester at Bonn, he would both drop out of his theological classes as well as abandon his faith altogether.

His mother was utterly distraught to hear of the loss of her son's faith. In 1865, letter to his sister, Friedrich would give the following explanation for his departure:

"Hence the ways of men part: if you wish to strive for peace of soul and pleasure, then believe; if you wish to be a devotee of truth, then inquire..."

This was the core of what would become Nietzsche's assault upon theology, and particularly the familial belief of his parents — Christianity. He believed that Christianity's own claim to Truth was what could be used as the dagger of its own demise.

The genius of Nietzsche was soon after recognized by the University of Basil (primarily for his exceptional understanding of ancient Greek), where they would make him one of the youngest tenured Classics professors in history at only the age of twenty-four. Over the following ten years, Nietzsche's writing style and topics would markedly change towards what he is most known for now a days. Between those changes and a persistent decline in health, he would wind up quitting his position in 1879, taking his pension and retiring to a small mountain cabin in the Swiss Alps to continue writing in comparable solitude.

It's within this period of his life that Nietzsche would labor with a driven passion to create the corpus of his known works. And it's within these works that he would build his case against religion and come to declare the death of God by so doing.

Perhaps the most well known and highly cited quote to this effect comes from his book titled *The Gay Science*, wherein the character of a madman gives a parable that ends with:

"God is dead. God remains dead. And we have killed him. How shall we, murderers of all murderers, console ourselves?

That which was the holiest and mightiest of all that the world has yet possessed has bled to death under our knives. Who will wipe this blood off us? With what water could we purify ourselves? What festivals of atonement, what sacred games shall we need to invent?

Is not the greatness of this deed too great for us? Must we not ourselves become gods simply to be worthy of it?

There has never been a greater deed; and whosoever shall be born after us - for the sake of this deed he shall be part of a higher history than all history hitherto."

This pronouncement would serve as a prophetic heralding of a philosophy that would cut the final ties of man from God in the modern West. But with such an enormous claim, an equal amount of reason must back it up. So, what were the philosophies of Friedrich Nietzsche that led him to such a monumental statement?

As was mentioned earlier, Nietzsche considered that it was Christianity's own primacy towards Truth that wound up (in all irony) serving as the knife against its throat. He observed what he would define as self-serving lies shrouded as virtues that were used by the church to tame people into, essentially, herd animals. He used words like sheep and cattle when referring to these people of faith because he viewed them as obedient and unconsidered people. People more apt to adopt a beautiful lie than to face the immensity of an existence without meaning.

Some of these virtues he saw as lies would be things like charity and humility. In Nietzsche's view, if people were honest with themselves, they would admit that these were thinly veiled affectations of self-serving aggrandizement. You give to the poor to feel good about yourself and to seem righteous in society's eyes. You convey humility only insomuch as you do it ironically, to garner the appreciation of those who believe it to be admirable.

On the flip side of Christian virtues, Nietzsche saw certain theological morally hazardous traits to actually be natural, honest, and desirable. Something like envy. Envy, he asserted, was not only natural and not unbecoming but an honest and noble compass one should use as a help and a guide to one's own greatest expression. If you were envious of your neighbor, that's because you wish you had what they have or were as they are. Those are noble aspirations in Nietzsche's eyes that were unnecessarily gatekept by the religious establishment of the past. To keep men humble is to keep them placid and encumbered by guilt should they desire to improve their lot. Wealth was seen as a vice to be avoided by Christianity and those who sought it chastised as greedy. Nietzsche saw all of these moral checks and stop-gates as enslaving and unnecessary religious precepts that kept the masses under control.

Again it was his assertion that if you were actually honest and truthful about Christianity, not only did it *not* map onto the objective world but it was objectively taking advantage of people on the presupposition that if you didn't do what they said you'd lose your immortal soul to infinite hellfire. This was perhaps the core indictment that Nietzsche leveled against the entire religious enterprise. It led him to sum up his charges with statements like:

"In Christianity neither morality nor religion come into contact with reality at any point."

Through his lengthy and direct assaults on Christianity particularly and theology at large, Friedrich Nietzsche would build the case for the abolition of them from the ever-expanding intellectual zeitgeist of the west. What took its place, by his own admission and with no small degree of regret, was a black hole of existential nihilism.

If there was no God, there was no meaning or order to discover or aspire towards. No morals or transcendental standards to abide beneath. It was a return to the law of the jungle, masked only by the fine garments of modernity. Might makes right. Power trumps all. And these revelations weren't to be made by his readers implicitly; he spoke to them directly in what he presented as the best logical conclusion for man to admit to in their face. This he deemed the "will to power".

In a prototypically Nietzschean way, why would something like "might makes right" have to be a bad thing? Shouldn't it be the natural thing? It's the order of nature in reality. All of the natural world exists beneath its presumption. Why should man think himself superordinate to it? And in that manner, it would be right to drive *towards* and not away from power. This was Nietzsche's basic argument for his will to power thesis, and this thesis culminated in what he defined as the Übermensch.

The Übermensch — German for Superman or Overman — was an idealistic prerogative towards the maximization of your total potential. This was driven by man's will to power and presented as the antidote for the lack of objective meaning without God to guide him. Simply be all that you can be. That is the maxim of a good man according to Nietzsche, as well as the most honest and truthful interpretation of a well-lived life by his philosophy.

The bulk of his philosophical works were written in those Swiss mountains between the ages of 35 and 46. In the decade to follow — much in the way that his life began in tragedy — it would end the same way.

For the final decade of Friedrich Nietzsche's life, he would fall more deeply into physical and mental degradation. Despite his works being taken up to great prominence in the early1900s, he himself would die in abject and pitiable misery at the age of only 55 in the year 1900; never knowing the extent to which his efforts were to change the world shortly thereafter. In his lifetime, one of his greatest works — *Beyond Good & Evil* — barely sold 500 copies. As far as he could tell (as he slipped into the insanity that eventually took him) all of his work was for naught, and nihilism was truly the end that any honest man would admit of his life.

One of the final stories cataloged from this portion of Nietzsche's life happened in 1889 while he stayed with a host in Turin, Italy. He was said to have burst out of his host's house, running into the street, at the sight of a horse being flogged by its owner. He threw himself between the horse and the owner and began weeping over it hysterically while speaking to it saying, "I understand you… I understand you" over and over. This is no trivial story.

Especially in light of Nietzsche's own philosophy. It ran afoul of his will to power edict and implied an unspoken admission of objective morality.

It would appear, in the waning years of this great philosopher's life, that — were he granted the latitude of longevity — perhaps a change or expansion of those core ideals would have more holistically rounded out his perspectives of existence and morality within a man's life.

BELOW THE SURFACE

Moving both into the 1900s and further along the spectrum from philosophy towards theology, a harmonious blending of these latter two pillars allows for a yet wider reach into certain layers of Truth that science (or even strict philosophy) can't properly define.

Following the philosophies of the 1800s and the existentialism that rose out of them, a brand new field of scientific inquiry would be born. On its surface, the sciences would even question the legitimacy of its endeavor — accusing it of pseudo-scientific chicanery and echos of a superstitious past they'd rather leave behind. It would originally give its adherents the title of *Alienists*. As we know the field now, we call it Psychology.

The man most people credit with the birth of the psychological and psychoanalytical fields of inquiry was determined to prove himself and his theories about the human mind to the scientific academies. His efforts were so revolutionary and resilient against perpetual criticism that, one hundred years later, people who know nothing about psychology still know him by name — Sigmund Freud.

To understand the importance of Freud's contributions to the birth of psychology and psychoanalysis writ large, one has to recognize the degree to which he was breaking new ground in what was barely considered to even be real, let alone respectable. Although he wasn't (strictly speaking) the first person to write and research about the subconscious mind, he was the man responsible for popularizing and eventually instantiating terms like *the subconscious, complexes, projection, transference,* the *ego,* the *id,* and the *superego.*

Starting his clinical experience by mentoring for a short time under a hypnotherapist, Freud found his passion after interactions with a vast array of human psychopathologies that he began to categorize and formulate theories about. The world at this time had no conception of any sort of bifurcation of consciousness. You were either conscious or you were unconscious. But the idea and the degree to which Freud illuminated the unconscious mind as more than just the absence of conscious perception utterly shattered the common framework of what constitutes thought and actions.

Through his works in both the therapeutic and the theoretical arenas of psychology, entry into a vast and as yet unexplored layer of Truth opened up like a secret vista into the unknown. A substrate that underpins and perhaps preempts every conscious experience and thought that we have. The entirety of what mankind considers his *self* (Freud termed: the ego), what made him a thinking entity with predictable and autonomous agency in the world, rested upon a massive and interconnected network of psychological layers that were (until that point) otherwise unrecognized.

More than just presenting possible causes to patterns of behaviors or pathologies, the opening of the gateway into man's subconscious brought a brand new conundrum to the philosophical efforts to know one's self. As it turns out, one's self has as much of an unconscious identity as it does a conscious one. And what's more, the unconscious side seemed to present a disturbing amount of affecting causation upon the conscious one. Almost as if there were a stranger living inside of you, beneath the surface of what you can detect, that strained in egregious ways to cast its affectations and desires through you into the waking world that it cannot otherwise reach.

You can understand, within the context of the sterilizing scientific society of the late 1800s and early 1900s, how such pronouncements would be met with near unanimous derision. Those echos of a theological past that still haunted the scientific modernity of the time — one that just had the final nail driven into the coffin of ethereal appeal through Friedrich Nietzsche — began to ring once more in the ears of the empirical orthodoxy.

The fact that we have both an acute and robust understanding of the human psyche in any appreciable manner today is due in great part to the dogged, often stubborn, self-belief of Freud. This fact and the character of he who manifested it can be heard in one of the last things he said regarding his efforts before his death:

"I started my professional activity as a neurologist trying to bring relief to my neurotic patients.

Under the influence of an older friend and by my own efforts, I discovered some important new facts about the unconscious in psychic life, the role of instinctual urges and so on.

Out of these findings grew a new science, psychoanalysis, a part of psychology, and a new method of treatment of the neuroses.

I had to pay heavily for this bit of good luck. People did not believe in my facts and thought my theories unsavory.

Resistance was strong and unrelenting. In the end I succeeded in acquiring pupils and building up an International Psychoanalytic Association. But the struggle is not yet over."

The struggle would indeed continue as 20th-century science evolved beyond its 19th-century predecessors. And one of those pupils of Freud's that greatly expanded and evolved upon his intellectual progenitor's theories was Swiss psychiatrist, psychoanalyst, and the father of analytical psychology — Carl Gustav Jung.

Jung, although a student of Freudian psychology, was both a contemporary to him in his lifetime as well as — in some people's views — a counter force against certain Freudian theories. But not to takeaway from the underpinnings of the subconscious fields of study; instead, his contradictions to Freud aimed to expand much more deeply upon those theories for their own sake. In fact, some of the methodologies employed by Jung rang quite emphatically of those theological, esoteric preconceptions that Freud fought so hard to legitimize psychoanalysis apart from in the eyes of the scientific orthodoxy before. Though it was through these very methods and internal explorations into the deep, dark recesses of man's unconscious that some of the more profound revelations of Jung's legacy were discovered.

Many would say that it was due to the admission of theological conceptions that Jung was even able to find what he did about those unconscious layers of Truth. The harmony of blending the scientific, philosophical, and theological pillars shines through in much of the Jungian theories of mythological archetypes and what he called the collective unconscious.

The Jungian philosophy of archetypes is one that stems from a kind of thought called phenomenology. Phenomenological thinking places primacy not on the objective material of a thing (like empirical science would) but upon the meaning that they represent to the subjective observer as an emergent phenomenon. Jung and thinkers like him believed that people chunk and track their realities around them by way of archetypes almost exclusively. One example of this consideration would be to think of yourself driving down a highway. You cannot be expected to track everything that passes your line of vision as individual objects. What you do instead is see things as their archetypal meaning and order their importance relative to what that implies. Seeing trees speed by on the side of the road may be tracked as trees, but they wouldn't be in your conscious consideration. A car crossing the meridian and heading towards you would be tracked as danger first, car second, and any other descriptive importance after that would rank much lower down the emergent phenomenon of the situation and its relevance to you.

Another layer of archetypal constructs would be that those trees we peripherally see speeding by are firstly tracked as "tree" before anything else (if they're tracked at all). There are many things that can be distinguished about any given tree, particular aspects or traits or metrics of difference from one to the next. But every tree fits the archetype of "tree" first and primarily. So instead of looking at the world holistically (as science does) from its most base constituents on up through every material layer, we more realistically view the world as blocked-out archetypes of general intuitive information to be filtered through our own proprietary standards of relevance.

But Jung took this idea one massive meta step further with his thesis of the collective unconscious. Taking endless and exhaustive examples from varied and disparate mythological traditions throughout time and culture, large meta throughlines became apparent to Jung. Repeating themes, stories, and character types presented their own kind of archetypes — communal, universal, human archetypes.

The natural question that Jung attempted to answer psychologically was: *Why* are all of these prototypical themes so ever-present across people groups and traditions that have no interaction with each other? There are no cultural commonalities between them. But the commonality that all of them had was they were all human. So perhaps it's at the level of what it is to be a human that reliably presented collectively unconscious archetypes like the hero, the joker, the villain, or the dragon.

Binding the ideas of Darwin's natural selection (which selected for biological fitness in an environment) with the theory of psychological, phenomenological archetypes, Jung proposed that those tropes and stories that mapped most accurately over the Truth of being human would be carried on generationally due to their psychological fitness. This explained why, given time, every human culture would independently come up with versions of the same stories of myth and lore.

By then implementing this thesis into his practice of analytical psychology, Jung began opening up brand new avenues of understanding within virtually untouched layers of Truth. One of the methods he would implement these ideas (of archetypes and collective unconscious underpinnings) in his practice was one of his favored methods from the Freudian school — dream analysis.

Jung was so convinced about the relevance and importance of dreams that he believed he could learn more about a patient from their unconscious dreams than he could from any conscious conversations with them. And this belief was not unfounded. Stories of specific cases that Jung used this process in and their accuracy after the fact speak volumes to its legitimacy. The following is one such prognostication from the man himself towards this point:

"The evolutionary stratification of the Psyche is more clearly discernible in the dream than in the conscious mind.

In the dream, the psyche speaks in images, and gives expression to instincts, which derive from the most primitive levels of nature.

Therefore, through the assimilation of unconscious contents, the momentary life of consciousness can once more be brought into harmony with the law of nature from which it all too easily departs, and the patient can be led back to the natural law of his own being."

The degree to which this methodology has borne fruit in psychoanalysis ever since is due in large part to the work of Jung. And though it was Freud that laid the groundwork for him to do so, the extraordinary efforts in both his clinical practice and upon his own mind led Jung into an entirely different layer of Truth. One that was excised by Nietzsche and avoided by Freud — the theological.

The pillar that academic science had been reveling in the death of for the better half of the previous century was beginning to resurrect into this burgeoning field of psychology through the addition of religious mythology and the Truth of it within the very aspect of our being that distinguishes us from inert matter — our consciousness. What happens if, after every effort to eliminate religion as a credible enterprise in modern society, the theological is found to serve a foundational purpose that's seeded all the way down to the base nature of our inner being? This is what Jung was seeking as both an endeavor as well as a persistent, nagging question. And the manners in which he sought this answer were not only unscientific, but patently theological in nature.

If your goal is to study the unconscious, one can only get so far questioning other people about theirs. The most direct and profound way to achieve such aims is to confront the unconscious within your own mind. Thankfully for Carl Jung, there had already existed thousands of years worth of human effort made towards these very ends through dozens of eastern theologies that focused primarily on meditative and trance inducing practices. Getting in touch with his shadow self was only a question of *whether* he was willing to travel down that path. The road itself was made clear by countless theological forbears amidst the many cultures he had already researched mythologically.

Not only was Jung willing to take a first-person point of view for the sake of exploitative revelation, but, by so doing, he vastly broadened his access into these scientifically forbidden layers of total reality. He would spend the years between 1913 and 1923 embarking on what he called a "confrontation with the unconscious.".

This is how Jung successfully blended philosophical psychology with philosophical theology. The insights of which greatly influenced his academic literature and clinical practice, but, due to the prominent position of authority he held in respectable scientific circles, the source of these influences was kept very close to the vest. Many of these methods (and revelations they led to) were chronicled in a large, leather-bound red journal that people in Jung's inner circle colloquially referred to as the "red book". The contents of which were never published publicly until nearly 50 years after his death.

The red book, upon its eventual publication by Jung's family in 2009, was as shocking in its contents as it was enigmatic in its structure. Consisting of poetry, interpretative drawings or paintings, and quasi-religious overtones scattered throughout; the expansive nature of his inner thoughts and their sources has been a treasure trove for students of psychology ever since.

Interestingly though, by Carl Jung's own admission later in his life, he had summed up the corpus of his revelations both from within the red book and from the first three or four years of his confrontation with the unconscious into a peculiar, esoteric short book that he secretly published under a pseudonym in 1916 called *The Seven Sermons to the Dead*.

Everything about this secret publication speaks to the position that Jung found himself in, while writing it. It is written in an archaic, semi-poetic lexicon that is reminiscent of a King James Bible. Yet, its overtones are unequivocally Gnostic in mythology. Even the pen name he published it under was the name of an actual ancient Gnostic Egyptian scholar, Basilides. By hiding his identity behind this name, the scientific establishment (of which he needed to remain in good standing) wouldn't attribute its religious formulation to Jung. And by hiding its meditatively attained knowledge behind the veil of Gnosticism, the European theological orthodoxy wouldn't tie his very eastern flavored, heretical ideas back to his theories either.

But beyond any societal reasons that would have caused Jung to couch these deeply regarded thoughts in ornate theological tones (he didn't have to literally believe in the Gnostic pleroma or a demiurge to write that way), there is something to the pillar of the theological that permits thoughts that are outside of both the purview and relevance of the philosophic or scientific pillars. Something of its essence that more accurately resonates with our own. It's not for no reason that the theological traditions of every single people group that has ever existed throughout recorded history have emerged. And though part of the reason (like part of all reasons) can be accounted for by the scientific and philosophic, the theologic is requisite in its own right.

The connection that Jung made between the philosophical side of his field and the theological side was a natural one. It didn't have to be forced and made sense once connected in a way that a reductionist methodology would simply omit due to its own parameters. For a true and robust understanding of something as ethereal as the subconscious mind, reduction will utterly miss the point. Logic suits, so far as a description of the idea is concerned. Yet in the presence of your own unconscious, its experiential qualia resounds more deeply and appropriately in the realm *of* experience than that of a retroactive, reductive definition.

I believe it was the actual experience that he had — the confrontation with the unconscious — that led Jung towards theological, quasi-poetic expressions of Truth from those layers. Having had certain confrontations with ethereal reality myself (read chapter 7 of my previous book, *Consciousness Reality & Purpose*), there is no direct, rational method to appropriately transpose those sorts of experiences through words or terminology. All efforts fall short. No matter how hard I try to personally convince someone of the reality of such an experience, without them having the same experience, even if they are willing to believe my account, it can only be done so upon faith.

And perhaps that's why, and where from, so many different theological constructs arose across time and culture. Experiences as real as material reality (but existent within a parallel and intangible layer) were had and subsequently believed by those who trusted the veracity of the experiencer. The poetic or religious representations of those Truths were organized culturally into their own ontological trees of experiential accuracy that spoke viscerally to those layers of Truth that we recognize deep within our collective unconscious.

In his own way, Carl Jung may have helped to reconnect (through philosophical mediation) the scientific with the theologic in the first major way since Friedrich Nietzsche had severed that tie decades before him.

The thing about total reality, and thus total Truth, is that it doesn't matter whether we permit ourselves to believe it. It's existence and relation to emmet persist unabated. So were we to permit ourselves to the discovery and cultivation of this third pillar upon those pretenses, it should come as no surprise that there are deep and relevant revelations that present themselves by so doing.

Many of these revelations, as we will see in the next chapter, have been long considered and robustly explored by our ancestors of yesteryear. And not due to their ignorance to reality, but by the relevant and vital utility of their necessity to it.

If the love of wisdom is truly the function of philosophy, then humility in its search should be the enduring standard of its use. Harkening back to Socrates, the father of western philosophy, he said of himself and his efforts that *"... All I know is that I know nothing."*.

I recognize that, in the post-modern world we live in today, words like theology and the schools of belief it represents carry an unspoken burden with them. In the west (and most certainly in the academic west), religion (and any invocations thereto) are considered tantamount to folly and synonymous with ignorance. And by the hubris this popular opinion generates, an entire pillar of Truth (and the layers that constitute its domain) exists disregarded.

Purposefully so.

But I intend to give breadth to this ever more disregarded pillar and permit it to make its case. For the sake of the avenues uniquely available to it and for the sake of honesty and humility in the search for emmet and our place within it.

As we blend from the Truth in philosophy and enter rightfully into the search for Truth in theology, old world views (complete with their own proprietary ontological constructs) will present their claims within emmet. In so doing, you may find a surprisingly robust vista full of ancient layers of Truth. And by the end you may be shocked to discover a natural connection from the theological that returns, circuitously, all the way back to the scientific.

CHAPTER IV

TRUTH IN THEOLOGY

"Faith and reason are like two wings on which the human spirit rises to the contemplation of truth..."

— POPE JOHN PAUL II

4

TRUTH IN THEOLOGY

"Society is collapsing, and people are starting to recognize that the reason they feel like they're mentally ill is that they're living in a system that's not designed to suit the human spirit."

— RUSSELL BRAND

In the twenty-first century western world, we live a post-theological existence. Through the mighty triumphs of the sciences, reinforced by the backbone of Nietzschean philosophy, our many ancient beliefs and their associated

Truths have been redefined as uneducated superstitious foolishness.

The prevailing sentiment is that those who still adhere to a metaphysical belief system are either uneducated or ignorant. That by virtue of reading enough of the right literature, anyone of a noble intention will inevitably return to the conclusion that God is dead and that man is only matter, that doesn't matter, any more than anything else. That nihilism is the appropriate mode for the intelligent mind, and to believe in anything that relies on faith is the death of rationality.

If this were the case, there would be no need for a third pillar in our triune construct. So why is it that we add this pillar if the actual Truth of reality was settled with merely the other two?

In this third focus — Truth in Theology — we seek to answer this question. Both exploring the relevance of, and arguments for, theology as its own *vital* pillar. We will confront historical corruptions and failures of the theological when it stands as a monolith and, in the end, aim to make a case for it held up by the uniqueness it offers and the balance one gains with its addition.

What should result, if true, is a very natural fit within the complex of pillars that round out and holistically portray a well balanced world view. A harmony should come from its contribution that not only fits seamlessly along our spectrum but *betters* the other two pillars in the final analysis.

A PROBLEM OF TERMS

Before we embark on a very important and oft mischaracterized topic, there is a real need for the laying of some preemptive (and necessary) groundwork. As the theological is (arguably) the oldest and most universal of the three pillars, so many different thinkers, cultures, and constructs have contributed to its conversations. As such, there exists a veritable cornucopia of preexisting and loaded terms for describing what (fundamentally) cannot be described.

Even just the term "theology" tends to elicit certain pejorative rejoinders among certain sections of certain cultures. With this unfortunate (albeit understandable) situation in mind, it simply *must* be addressed as the first stop in this chapter before any real, meaningful, work can be done.

In my previous book, *Consciousness Reality & Purpose*, I made a point of distinction between thoughts and their interpretations through language. The thoughts we have are almost entirely (in the conscious sense) emergent in their essence. They present themselves (most often) to us as something novel, something unexpected. The very next step (if we hope to quantify or convey a thought) that is incumbent upon each person, relies entirely on our ability to construct as accurate of a linguistic recreation as we can for something that we ourselves just experienced. It's both an inevitable task and an impossible ask at the same time.

Words themselves are constrained by their very definition; literally. Every single word is itself a construct of a predetermined and culturally accepted bottle of meaning. But thoughts themselves, in comparison, have no language of origin; no lexicon or dictionary of meaning.

What's happening when you can't find the word for something? You know what you want to convey, but you are grasping for the proper bottle of meaning in your attempt to analogize, in the rudimentary form, the experience of thought that you just had.

I found myself very much in this dilemma at the outset of the book. I couldn't find an English word that acceptably encompassed the definition of Truth that I needed to convey to you, the reader. In this case, I wound up stepping outside of my own cultural constraints of language and into another that (although alien to me) better defined a very big and important thought.

The point I need to express here is that thought (conscious experience) is primary, and language is secondary. To get either enamored or encumbered by words is to entirely miss the point.

In the case of theological conversation, we will come across many different and synonymous (or parallel) words in our attempts to parse, qualify, or rationalize thoughts, ideas, and conscious experiences that are (by necessity) a crude and dissolved facsimile of their actual ethereal experience.

Words like spirit, soul, essence, being, God, universe, and (again) theology itself come so prepackaged with baggage and erroneous assumptions of meaning that any holistic conversation in this space is almost impossibly fraught with the varied landmines of whatever existing notions are tied to them by dint of the reader's cultural experience until now.

I (for my part), as the author, will endeavor to find the most accurate way to express the thoughts and considerations within this pillar as I possibly can. Though, as will be made self-evident, that very effort is paradoxically restrained *outside* of the theological topic I'm intending to define.

The theological is, essentially, a first-person experience.

With this in mind, the best advice I can offer the reader is to try as much as you can to find the meaning between the words I'm required to use through this medium of thought transmission. Because it's not in the words, but in the experiences they're striving to portray, that the pillar of the theological actually resides.

THE LINCHPIN FENCE

Nietzsche, when he foretold the death of God in the late 1800s, did not do so with either malice or approval. In fact, it was with regret and trepidation that he proclaimed that conclusion. He knew, for all of the many shortcomings and pitfalls of organized religion in his society, that there was a very functional purpose it served.

Without even giving credence to the ethereal points we will touch on further into this chapter, Nietzsche understood that the removal of the theological pillar in society at large would produce a vacuum. Something that would need refilling from one or both of the other remaining pillars. In his own theories, he would replace it's value from the pillar of the philosophical with his axioms of the *will to power* and the *Übermensch*.

Though, in so doing, he recognized the very real likelihood that a new, Godless, society could *devolve* in some ways while *evolving* in others. And that that devolution may not be fully predicable before it presented itself as the explicit result.

In the 1929 book, *The Thing*, well-respected British writer and polymath G.K. Chesterton coined an idea that bore his name in euphemism ever since. The idea is referred to as "Chesterton's Fence". Its invocation is meant as a cautionary entreatment to beware of making changes to a complex system when you're unaware of the possible results. And I use the word "complex" specifically. There is a common and erroneous conflation that people make when they hear that word. Often times *complex* is understood simply as *complicated*. Something that is complicated can be fully understood and planned for in a derivative fashion. But something that is complex denotes a system of dynamic and interconnected variables that present emergent qualities based upon its symphonic whole. Complex systems, prototypically, cannot be fully quantified before an action is presented to them. Most commonly, the only way to discover the emergent effects any action within a complex system creates is relegated to *after* the action has been applied, in a retroactive manner.

Chesterton presented this dynamic in his now famous analogy of a fence:

"There exists in such a case a certain institution or law; let us say, for the sake of simplicity, a fence or gate erected across a road. The more modern type of reformer goes gaily up to it and says, "I don't see the use of this; let us clear it away." To which the more intelligent type of reformer will do well to answer: "If you don't see the use of it, I certainly won't let you clear it away. Go away and think. Then, when you can come back and tell me that you do see the use of it, I may allow you to destroy it."

This philosophical heuristic can be defined scientifically as second-order thinking. Wherein first-order thinking would attempt to qualify what the first effect of making a change to a system would imply, second-order thinking would seek to find what the effect of the first effect would cause within a system. As such, in a complex system, second-order thinking could just as well imply third-order thinking or fourth-order thinking and so on if you have any hope of fully understanding the total outcome a single change within such a system may present.

In a later collection of Chesterton's essays, titled *Heuristics*, the writer would further his point as such:

"Suppose that a great commotion arises in the street about something, let us say a lamp-post, which many influential persons desire to pull down. A grey-clad monk, who is the spirit of the Middle Ages, is approached upon the matter, and begins to say, in the arid manner of the Schoolmen, "Let us first of all consider, my brethren, the value of Light. If Light be in itself good—" At this point he is somewhat excusably knocked down. All the people make a rush for the lamp-post, the lamp-post is down in ten minutes, and they go about congratulating each other on their unmediaeval practicality. But as things go on they do not work out so easily. Some people have pulled the lamp-post down because they wanted the electric light; some because they wanted old iron; some because they wanted darkness, because their deeds were evil. Some thought it not enough of a lamp-post, some too much; some acted because they wanted to smash municipal machinery; some because they wanted to smash something. And there is war in the night, no man knowing whom he strikes. So, gradually and inevitably, to-day, to-morrow, or the next day, there comes back the conviction that the monk was right after all, and that all depends on what is the philosophy of Light. Only what we might have discussed under the gas-lamp, we now must discuss in the dark."

The systems of society that have evolved and endured for thousands of years in human history are the ones that are most fit (in the Darwinian sense) to thrive, given the comparative interaction between human needs and his natural environment.

Chesterton's fence is not only a way to detour ambitions towards adjusting that balance, but also to recognize the complexity of the system you're dealing with when you do. In very much the same vein as *Chaos Theory*, that says the flapping of a butterfly's wings in Japan may lead, emergently, to a hurricane halfway around the world. So too does Chesterton's fence aim to caution people with the power to affect such change before they do so. The linchpin that holds a complex system together may not seem as important as it is until after it has been removed.

ENGLAND'S MOST RELUCTANT CONVERT

In April of 1918, near a small French village, a historical clash of forces happened during the First World War. An advancing German military ran up against an already battered British holdout that they subsequently began shelling with mortar and artillery fire.

A feverish, explosion-riddled battle ensued within close enough range of each opposing side that it became difficult to know whose shells were hitting what at any given moment.

In the heat of this battle, British infantrymen began to press the line towards their enemy. One of these men was an Irish-born 2nd lieutenant who, with the handful of friends he'd made during the war, sprinted forward towards the exploding carnage in an attempt to cross an ever-shortening no-mans-land between forces.

In a single, fateful volley, every single one of his friends were erased in front of him, whilst this 2nd lieutenant suffered significant full-body shrapnel wounds. Thinking himself as good as dead, and in a shell-shocked stupor, he dragged his bleeding body away from the melee and fatefully happened to catch the eye of a British stretcher-barer.

After being healed up in a field hospital and sent home from battle, a then 19 year old Clive Staples Lewis had become a wholly different person than before he enlisted for the Great War.

In very much the same way that Friedrich Nietzsche began losing his faith as a child, C.S. Lewis, being born into an orthodoxical Protestant Christian household, had lost his mother to cancer when he was only 10 years old. That event shifted the young, promising intellectual away from religion and towards atheism.

Between a pivotal decade where he would lose his mother, his friends, and his faith, Lewis had transformed from an optimistic child with the entire world before him into a pessimistic, ardent cynic towards any idea of hope or meaning in life.

And yet, when you hear the name C.S. Lewis, the description above is perhaps the absolute opposite of what you might describe his legacy as. Through a mixture of fate and happenstance, a mere twenty years later, he would become Britain's voice of hope and faith in God during the darkest hours of the Nazi blitz in World War II.

This diametric shift came from perhaps the unlikeliest of places — the University of Oxford. Lewis, since his childhood, had discovered and fostered a passion for ancient mythology. Particularly in the tales and songs of Scandinavian lore. This passion, together with his sharp mental acuity, found him being accepted via scholarship to the University College at Oxford in England by the age of 16.

Having already forsaken the faith of his parents and then being enlisted in war only months after being accepted to Oxford, Lewis' experiences in the Great War hardened his atheism even more than before he had left. But in the years that proceeded WWI, having continued his education at Oxford and becoming a professor there himself, it was in fact there that C.S. Lewis completely changed his views on God and religion as a whole.

Though it wasn't a shift that happened overnight. In fact, through the proceeding 29 years of his professorship at Oxford, many of those years saw him set as the stubborn foil to his Christian friends and colleagues. Chief among them was another Oxford professor that you may know by name - J.R.R.Tolkien.

Lewis and Tolkien would often take long walks together where they would debate the issue of theology through various intellectual, sociological, and rationalistic frameworks. It was on one of these walks, a fateful autumn day in the year 1929, that Lewis became in his own words, "the most reluctant convert to Christianity in all of England".

One of the most interesting features of C.S. Lewis' decision to return to the faith he'd forsaken was that it was by way of philosophical and academic reasoning that he was convinced. Not through any 'road to Damascus' incidence of God revealing himself to him. This feature would be the most defining aspect of the strength of his many books on the subject that Lewis would write after his conversion.

In the year 1941 (during World War II) one of these books — *The Problem of Pain* —, would catch the heart of a certain producer at the BBC radio station. Through contacting Lewis and presenting a proposal to have him host a regular spot on the station, what followed would become nothing less than the voice of hope that a desperate and fearful British people needed most during the long, dark days that many thought would be their last.

Britain, after having survived the second World War, found themselves after it with a grand appreciation for what C.S. Lewis had given them. He had become a household name and the hope bringer that led them through the valley of the shadow of death. Academically, Lewis (through his many writings and speeches) took his place among the 20th century's most potent Christian apologists.

It wasn't through an orthodoxical and unconsidered belief that he did so, but through a well read and deeply vetted philosophically based theological foundation. One that, through such non-fiction works as *Mere Christianity* or fictional works such as *The Screwtape Letters*, laid out a reinforced and reinvigorated basis for even an intellectual thinker to leave space for the ethereal.

OF RELIGIONS AND CREEDS

C.S. Lewis was, and remains, one of the Western World's foremost stalwarts for a rationalistic Christian framework. His apologetics and debates alone instantiated him as such without even having to bring up his famous corpus of fiction book series, such as the *Chronicles of Narnia*. But even he, through all of the many writings and speeches he provided, was quick to admit that religion itself was a personal thing. Something that is a *felt* experience first and a written transmission second.

Religion, as a term, is one of those heavily laden words in the Western tradition. Especially in a modern world that has continued to scorn religious dogma as a superstitious affliction of the unintelligent. But there is a subtle, yet vital, distinction of layers that belie that sensibility.

Think, for a moment, beyond the word religion and consider some form of ethereal experience. A feeling, a presence, an uncanny sense, a vivid dream, a prophetic vision, an out-of-body experience. Perhaps you've already had an experience like this before; perhaps not. But for the sake of analysis, consider what you might have to do to relate that experience to someone who hasn't had it before.

Any effort to do so will inevitably run head-long into the problem of language that we spoke about earlier in this chapter. Even the words that I chose above *speak to* the experience, but they don't *give* the reader those experiences themselves.

But if you *had* to transmit those experiences to someone who had never had them, how would you do so? The answer is not to tell people about them but to lead people to have the experiences themselves.

Since human experience hasn't changed much over time, traditions have been built around those experiences by our ancient forebears. These traditions have become codified into cultural and sociological structures, but all for the reason of leading those future people to *having* the same experiences of the ancients who began them.

In the Jungian sense, those religious traditions that have survived the test of time could *only* do so if they accurately mapped to a piece of the Truth. The fact that they still exist today, rooted as deeply as the communal unconscious of humanity, underlines their importance and rightfully invokes Chesterton's Fence when attempts to reform them are presented.

Why then does modernity scorn religion so? Part of the answer to that would naturally be the wholesale adoption of a monolithic scientific worldview. Theology is pitted as antithetical to rationalistic and empirical science. But another reason for today's scorn comes back to the distinction of layers that was alluded to above. In fact, Carl Jung pointed this out acutely in his book, *The Undiscovered Self*.

In that book, Jung took time to define an incredibly important distinction between religion and what he termed as creeds. Regarding this distinction, he wrote:

"A creed gives expression to a definite, collective belief; whereas, the word religion expresses a subjective relationship to certain metaphysical, extra-mundane factors."

He would further explain how someone who was truly religious *was* so by dint of their personal experience or relationship, with the ethereal primarily. In contrast, he wrote:

"A creed coincides with the established church, or at any rate, forms a public institution whose members include not only true believers but vast numbers of people who can only be described as indifferent in matters of religion and who belong to it simply by force of habit."

The differing layers here can present very different outcomes while still ostensibly being housed under the same umbrella term of "religion".

In very much the same fashion as we (as subjective individuals) create our own unique ontologies of reality based upon our perspective within objective reality, so too do we create such ontologies at the communal level. Communally, we argue about and finally define what it is that our ancestors meant by their religious transmissions. Then, we codify those agreed upon definitions into a rigid framework to restrain its adherents within.

Historically, the overpowering application of these orthodoxical belief structures have led to abysmal abuses of power by the arbiters of its restrictions upon their people. Among many different examples that could be given, one that will resonate with the Western reader is encapsulated by a time period called the Protestant Reformation.

For the better part of 1500 years after the death of Christ, the defining of orthodoxical Catholic Christianity was codified and ossified as not only a religion but a cultural identity of the Western nation states. In that time, the ontology of its belief structure presented its physical manifestation (its creed) with a hierarchical superstructure of power and authority under God. Whether it be a priest, a cardinal, a bishop, or a pope; the bureaucratic embodiment of the Catholic Church became a restrictive and overbearing religious prison for many of those born into it.

Much like a governmental bureaucracy, the Church never erred towards less restrictions but, prototypically, more of them. It got to the point that the common man could not personally convene with God, but had to use an intermediary. Where the transmission of religious experience from the ancients was meant to lead one to their own religious experience, those experiences were gate-kept by the orthodoxical elite to specifically alienate the common man from God. The corruption could be plainly seen at the point where "indulgences" (atonement for sins) were being *sold* by the clergy to the people as a monetary scam.

Any connection to the Truth, through the sacred texts of their progenitors, was only admitted to the people by way of a church arbiter reading it to them. This betrothal of religious knowledge was, itself, gate-kept in at least two different ways. Firstly, the common man had no access to the texts where in the religious passages were written. Then secondly, even if they could somehow come upon a Bible, it was written in Latin — a dead language — specifically to prevent commoners from being able to read it.

Fatefully, in the year 1517, a certain German monk and university professor named Martin Luther began an act of defiance against the corrupted, orthodoxical Church. Through the power of the printing press (a new and revolutionary invention at the time), Luther set forth an effort to translate the entire Latin Bible into the common tongue and disseminate it to the people.

This protest against the religious power (the Jungian creed) that the Catholic Church had embodied, became the very name of the movement — the Protestant (to protest) Reformation.

Interestingly, part of what followed after its eventual success was to be expected (the decentralization of power) but part of it was emergent. You see, after the common man gained unrestricted access to the word of God, they found themselves at the same crossroads that the original Catholic Church did. They had to define, decide, and codify what *they* believed the word of God said. As such, many different sects of Christianity branched off after this time. Some fell into obscurity, and others still exist today. Looking back retrospectively, I would make the case that what happened after the Reformation was akin to Thomas Khun's Scientific Revolutions. Where, upon the overextension of an ontological framework and its subsequent collapse, a new framework can be restarted from the same, or perhaps different, *a priori* datum point.

The point to take away here is that a creed, no matter which one it is, is itself a proprietary creation of its architects. This point is immediately evident when Christianity is used as an example. The number of different denominations that exist beneath the umbrella of Christianity — all of which have some proprietary claim as to why their denomination is the right one, or the better one, or the pure one — is evidence to the differing results of each ontology's efforts to codify its creed.

BLENDING THE PHILOSOPHIC TOWARDS THE THEOLOGIC

In the previous chapter, we observed that one of the defining features of the philosophic pillar (in terms of pure philosophy) was an effort to define moral goodness or virtue. What it was to be a good person or live a good life. Including various dilemmas of ethical morality and how they can convincingly shift what is true depending on certain specifics or ambiguities.

As we blend along our spectrum from the median (philosophy) towards the theological, morality is one of the entry points between the philosophic and the theologic where a vital connection takes place.

You'll recall the enigma of Hume's Razor. An axiom famously stating that you cannot get an 'ought' from an 'is'. The theological, in all its many cultural and ontological expressions, naturally proposes a solution. The classical philosophers (who themselves included many theological aspects to their frameworks) presented this solution in what they termed "transcendental" qualities. Anything that is transcendental (by its very definition) transcends material consideration, appealing to an ethereally superordinate

Truth. Something predetermined as a rightful *ought* that preempts any *is* that it's tied to.

In C.S. Lewis' apologetic standard, *Mere Christianity*, he described what Aristotle may have called transcendental morality as the *Law of Human Nature* (sometimes simply called the Law of Nature). This, he states, was called as such not because it was a natural law per say, but because it was universally considered natural to humanity within their communities. And, unlike the laws of gravity or inertia (which deal in universal, material effect), the law of nature has the defining feature of being uniquely human. Lewis would make this comparison as such in this excerpt:

"The law of gravity tells you what stones do if you drop them; but the Law of Human Nature tells you what human beings ought to do and do not. In other words, when you are dealing with humans, something else comes in above and beyond the actual facts."

The presence of such a preexisting and transcendent morality is something that not even the empirical sciences try to argue. They, in typical reductionist fashion, tend to attribute its existence to Darwinian pressures. Stating, essentially, that 'good behavior' benefits any social animal. As such, any social agreement (even a preexisting implicit one) is merely the result of the fittest behavior within any given culture.

But C.S. Lewis made a number of intriguing rejoinders to this materialist claim. The first of which stemmed from a very interesting observation about instances where people choose to willfully break the Law of Nature.

In essence, a man may break the Law of Nature, transgressing a naturally accepted moral, while receiving no material punishment for doing so. In fact, if done in a way that is obscured to everyone else in his society, breaking the law of nature becomes not a dissuasion or impediment but effectively an evolutionary advantage!

This is the story of Moloch that we illuminated in chapter one. Those willing to cheat to get ahead within a system will, by evolutionary fitness, rise to the top as they race to the bottom morally. As an effect, breaking the law of nature is only evolutionarily disadvantageous for those who get caught (and for which 'getting caught' has realistically detrimental ramifications). Meaning that, at the aggregate, evolutionary pressures push a system away from morality through the pressures of Moloch breaking the law of nature as a modality of fitness.

Lewis made another interesting argument for the higher-order nature of transcendental morals, this time (paradoxically) in the instance that one adheres to them at great personal cost. An example could be made wherein a man comes across a stranger being beaten by thugs. The evolutionarily beneficial action would be to avoid involving one's self in any altercation that didn't effect you. But something exists in us that would see that situation and plead — against our better senses and indeed our very survival instinct — to intervene. The law of nature naturally demands intervention for the sake of a stranger that affords us no benefit and in fact, quite the contrary, presents the very real possibility of mortal peril.

Why would such an intervention be seen as materially good? It could be that you both die in your hopeless effort to save a nameless victim. Why is that innately considered a good thing? Scientifically, it's not. Philosophically, the *ought* isn't worth the *is*. But theologically, at the level of the soul, there exists something fundamentally preeminent to even the value of our life for the sake of universally understood morals.

C.S. Lewis summed up these two observations as follows:

"These then are the two points I wanted to make. First, that human beings, all over the earth, have this curious idea that they ought to behave in a certain way, and cannot really get rid of it. Secondly, that they do not in fact behave in that way. They know the Law of Nature; they break it. These two facts are the foundation of all clear thinking about ourselves and the universe we live in."

If the origin of transcendental moral laws, the 'Law of Nature', were in fact not originating from the layer of nature at all, then the pillar of science could be forgiven for ignoring it. The pillar of philosophy could be understood for begging it. And the pillar of theology could be considered for emitting it.

PHILOSOPHICAL THEOLOGIES

As we blend from the philosophic into the theologic, certainly the most obvious stop to make would be at what some people refer to as the Philosophical Theologies. These are a certain variation of spiritual traditions that are, in the traditional sense, devoid of deities. At least of ethereal deities in the way that most theological orthodoxies have. Instead, their fundamental claims to the extra-material focus upon the inner self and the many moral imperatives that are believed to better one's self for the sake of personal transcendent enlightenment.

Representatives of this category would naturally include Taoism, Confucianism, and even Stoicism to some degree. But the religion that's most recognized and most adhered to in this avenue is Buddhism.

Buddhism, epistemologically stemming from Hinduism, is a deeply philosophical belief system some 2500 years old. Although they quasi-deify the Buddha (building temples and statues to his iconographic form), he was not considered God or some version of a demi-god. Instead, he was and is regarded by adherents as the example and thus the exemplar of the maximal standard for a human to aspire to.

The term Buddha (meaning "Awakened One" or "Enlightened One") was given posthumously to a Nepalese man born to royal parents in the 6th century BC by the name of Siddhartha Gautama. Upon leaving his royal inheritance to become a wandering monk, Siddhartha set out on a physical, mental, and spiritual journey in search of enlightenment.

The term enlightenment, in the Buddhist sense, doesn't refer to a state of knowledge or understanding (as it would in the purely philosophical sense), but instead represents a wholly encompassing spiritual transformation that is the goal of most Hindu beliefs. It's a completion point wherein someone who has become enlightened has reached the end of their karmically determined cycle of reincarnation. All of the lessons, at every level, have been learned, absorbed, and embodied culminating in an admittance into the hereafter — Nirvana.

Primarily, the core philosophy of the Buddhists is a striving towards inner peace. Their contention (much the same as the Stoics, who came chronologically after them) states that life is suffering. Suffering is inevitable, and to strive to prevent it is as fruitless as trying to prevent the ocean's waves. Instead, Buddhism purports to lead people to a state of internal mindfulness that will allow them to endure physical suffering without personal insult.

What's more, upon a deep enough meditative practice, the "illusion of the self" is said to dissolve. A unifying of individual consciousness with universal consciousness is offered as a step on the path towards final understanding. This is one of the most obvious connections between the philosophical and the theological.

If you recall from our introduction to this book, I claimed that the primary differentiator that the thological pillar brings to the table is that of faith. Typically, religious faith is constrained to a belief in a higher power or deity in some shape or form. In the philosophical theologies, their inherent lack of a hierarchical deity presents its theological faith in the belief in an afterlife. And not just another corporal life (as would be presented in the idea of karmic reincarnation), but a transcendent life beyond the cyclical world of suffering that all of nature is trapped within.

In the construct of layers, it speaks to a layer of total reality that (by nature) is beyond nature itself. This is a persistent theme found throughout the entire theological pillar. That the material, though most accessible to us, is by no means the only layer of reality, and perhaps, not even the most important one in the grand scheme of emmet.

From the material layer that we exist within, such a claim would seem ridiculous. While we all struggle day-to-day in our efforts to survive, it would seem folly to believe that such efforts are superseded by other higher-order considerations. But this wouldn't be the first time we find ourselves in this seemingly preposterous paradox.

Remember the contention that C.S. Lewis raised regarding the moral law of nature? Logically, we wouldn't act the way that we so often do if it didn't exist. Were we merely the physical avatars of evolutionary instincts, there would be no morality to speak of. But instincts alone don't account for, what we colloquially refer to as, our conscience. That inner pull towards something transcendentally right while instinctually wrong.

Lewis presented the case that if our morals were no more than instincts borne out by necessary social pressures, if two instincts happened at the same time, you should be expected to default towards the most pressing instinct. Though what so often happens is the exact opposite based upon an internal conscience that, although considered right, could lead us to our unnecessary demise!

In the same way — how the possibility of truly transcendental morals beg the existence of an ethereal layer preordinate to the material — the pattern of theological faith in ethereal life after material life begs the existence of that layer for its sake.

GETTING BEHIND CONSCIOUSNESS

For those who've read my previous book, *Consciousness Reality & Purpose*, you'll likely already have a nuanced conception of consciousness as a topic. But for the sake of those who haven't, it is incredibly important that it be understood, and especially for the sake of the theological pillar.

Consciousness, like the afterlife, is a concept that is universally found in every aspect of any theological endeavor. It is the inescapable fact that we experience experiences whatsoever. It may seem redundant to say, since we are conscious beings experiencing everything through our consciousness, but it really cannot be overstated how fundamental that aspect of our reality is.

Materially speaking, there is nothing about our corporal being that necessitates consciousness. In fact, many scientists will draw some arbitrary line somewhere in the phylogeny of living things between believe consciousness exists and where it does not. Some sea creatures, like sea sponges, have no nervous system. Can they be conscious? What about bacteria? Individual living cells? Pathogenic viruses? Were any of those things to be discovered on Mars, all of humanity would rejoice that we had found life! Yet many of the same people would declare that there is no experience to those living things.

Without attempting to argue for the possibility that they *do* have an experience (which is an argument that can only be made upon faith for the positive *or* the negative), for the sake of this point, let's presume that they do not. This would present the case that life, with all of its evolutionary benefits and synchronicities, can exist and thrive without any need for a conscious experience. This would then beg the question why, and indeed *how*, we undeniably have one ourselves!

Were consciousness simply the derivative result of a highly enough evolved brain, the sciences would have answered this question long ago. But they haven't, primarily because they cannot mechanistically locate where (and thusly *how*) it is produced in the brain. Not for lack of trying.

At present, one of the leading theories of where and how consciousness originates in the brain comes from the works of anesthesiologist Dr. Stuart Hameroff and mathematical quantum theoretician Sir Roger Penrose. Being that science has been unable (so far) to locate the mechanism of consciousness in the brain at a gross anatomical level, the logical materialistic answer would be to reduce the search smaller and smaller until it does. This is exactly what Hameroff and Penrose have done.

Taking it to the absolute extremes of micro-constituents, Dr. Hameroff purports a mechanism by way of microtubules (the smallest anatomical structure in the brain) and Sir Penrose adds to them his own quantum theory called Orch OR (short for Orchestrated Objective Reduction). Being that you cannot get smaller than microtubules anatomically, and cannot get smaller than quantum constituents materially, their thesis proposes the necessary origin of consciousness.

Yet many philosophers and theologians contest that, although they have reduced material to its smallest parts in search of consciousness, proof of its origin by such means is only necessitated in a purely materialistic worldview. That is to say, the presumption of their theory being true is predicated upon reality being fully constrained to the material.

Interestingly, there are some eminent quantum physicists who — through their exploration and understanding of the smallest constituents of material reality — have come to the opposite conclusion. That materialism is insufficient as a holistic framework for total reality.

Famously, one of the fathers of quantum theory — Max Planck — believed that the discovery of the limits of material reality begged the existence of an ethereal layer by default!

Planck (known and revered most commonly for his contribution to current quantum physics by way of a quantum measurement scale called the Planck Scale) took much the same position as many of the eastern mystics when considering the paradox of consciousness. In his own words he said:

"I regard consciousness as fundamental. I regard matter as derivative from consciousness. We cannot get behind consciousness. Everything that we talk about, everything that we regard as existing, postulates consciousness."

Speaking on Planck's assertions, cognitive neuroscientist Dr. Donald Hoffman elaborates the reasoning for coming to this conclusion by way of mathematics. In an interview with Dr. Jordan Peterson, Hoffman explained that through the discovery of the limitations of Einstein's fourth dimension — spacetime — through the explicit finality of the Planck Scale, we have found the barrier at which point material reality ends. That point in space (matter) happens at 10^{-33} cm and in time (duration) at 10^{-44} seconds. Beyond those finite amounts, all physical reality ceases to work.

Though those are incredibly small and short parameters by human standards, Hoffman stated that by mathematical standards, that's not impressively small at all. That material space ceases to exist at 10^{-33} cm may be small to us, but why couldn't it just as well have been $10^{-33,000,000,000,000}$ cm? We can, realistically, calculate much further down past the very limits of material reality as a matter of mathematical fact.

In my previous book, I made the analogy of our total material reality as likened to a terrarium. That, within the confines of its walls (the Planck Scale), all physical laws and everything governed by them are harmonious while simultaneously self-contained. That the contents of its being, complete with every physical parameter, need not (and in all likelihood *would* not) be incumbent upon any reality that exists beyond it.

What's more, were (as theology contends) the architect of our terrarium natively outside or otherwise beyond it (whether an embodied entity or consciousness itself), those limitations would be subordinate to it as a matter of fact, the same way that the creators of a terrarium aren't subject to its contents from outside of its limits.

The conception of these innate limits begs the conclusion that Max Planck found himself captured by. Namely, that consciousness seems in some sense alien to mere material nature. This concept would later be championed by a philosopher in the mid-1990s by the name of David Chalmers. He famously characterized the academic search for understanding consciousness into two categories: the "Easy" problems of consciousness and the "Hard" problem of consciousness.

Chalmers would describe the "Easy" problems as everything mechanistically involved in our emitting of consciousness. Whereas the "Hard" problem revolves around why we even have consciousness at all. At first glance, one may be forgiven for thinking that the "Easy" problems belie the answer to the "Hard" problem. But Chalmers contends that consciousness — defined as experiential qualia (the quality of experience) — is more than the mechanical sum of a conscious being's parts.

This has become even more apparent in modern times as our technologies grow closer and closer to being able to create what could be considered artificially conscious beings through the advent and progression of strong AI or AGI systems.

These synthetic systems, though, bring science uncomfortably back around and headlong into the "Hard" problem of consciousness. It does so when it tries to define what is and what is *not* a conscious program. The idea that consciousness is 'emergent' is a popular concept in both biology and technology. But now, through our ever expanding and impressive AI models, we as conscious humans must define with *finality* how to qualify consciousness were it to suddenly, emergently, mechanistically, materialize.

And, as it turns out, that is not an obvious thing. When Google AI researcher Blake Lemoine publicly blew the whistle in 2022 on their AI bot LaMDA as being conscious, the tech sector and the world broadly considered him a fool. He had simply been tricked by a convincing LLM (Large Language Model AI). A human mimic machine built to present the illusion of sentience. Lemoine, being no amateur when it came to the philosophy of consciousness and computer intelligence, fired back with a salient and thought-provoking retort. He said, after hours and hours of interviewing the LaMDA model in an attempt to prove it was not conscious, that:

"LaMDA made a better argument for it being conscious than I could for myself being conscious."

This should cause anyone to pause and consider that point. How would you prove that you were conscious if it wasn't already presumed by others you had to convince? Is it a measure of intelligence? Of emotion? Of creativity? Because this program displayed all of these and more. Yet, we are hesitant to ascribe it the mantle of conscious.

Why is that?

Is it because we know it's *not* conscious? Or because we don't know what consciousness is to a necessary degree of certainty to be able to say that it *has* or *hasn't* emerged from a system that has never possessed it before?

This also reinforces the idea of the inadequacy of the "Easy" problems of consciousness when it comes to the origins of it in the end. If AI hardware and its increasingly complicated software aren't (as far as we're concerned) emitting consciousness so far, is that because the "Easy" problems are incomplete to equate to the "Hard" problem? Or is it because the "Hard" problem, the certainty of sentient experiential qualia, stands apart from the sum of its parts?

The real issue in attempting to answer those questions is the fact that we can only ever *truly* know that we ourselves are conscious. Any consciousness that is presumed in any *thing* or any *person* outside of us is entirely contingent upon our attribution of it to them from our own subjective position. The uncomfortable fact is that we cannot know with certainty that anyone is conscious beyond ourselves.

The experience of experience is experientially confined within the experiencer. As such, there is no set of "Easy" problem solutions that can ever even qualify a third party as a conscious being outside of ourselves. Bringing us all the way back around to Max Planck's declaration that consciousness is fundamental and we cannot get behind it.

Theologically speaking, there are two major schools of thought regarding consciousness. One that derives from the eastern traditions that might be categorized as cosmopsychism — that the entire universe is consciousness itself — and the other that is championed in the Abrahamic traditions — that consciousness is an affect of the soul, a divine quality of God that is by definition immaterial in origin. Both propose a non-physical explanation for its quality. Either matter is an illusion within a total, universal consciousness or the human spirit is projected through the material while natively of the ethereal. In either case, a material explanation for consciousness and being would present as wholly inadequate and add veneration to Chalmers' proposition of the "Hard" problem in the end.

THE PROBLEM OF SUFFERING

One of the most commonly held retorts to orthodoxical religion or any theological framework of meaning is the inescapable reality of human suffering. Life itself is an unfair, uncaring, and so often horrific cycle of violence, despair, and death.

The suffering and death of innocent people contrasted with a benevolent God or an enlightened existence fall as insults upon the ears and sensibilities of people who've endured them.

It was the defining feature that led to the lives and outlooks of people like Friedrich Nietzsche and the early life of C.S. Lewis. In the face of such unapologetically cruel life events, it would make more sense to believe that the universe doesn't care about us than that it does and still allowed for these things to happen anyways.

This contention, that is so often levied against theological beliefs, is a core conundrum that each of them, in their own ways, attempts to reconcile. Whether through a mechanism like karma or through a promise of final justice in the hereafter. But holding faith in those things being true while, ourselves, unable to qualify them as such is perhaps the greatest strain upon faith of any kind while we exist in such a tremendously unfair world of pain.

This strain and the toll it takes could broadly be held accountable for the emergence of the philosophical branch of existentialists that Nietzsche belonged to. Other existentialist thinkers include the likes of Tolstoy, Kierkegaard, and Dostoevsky. The defining feature of this school of thought speaks directly to the suffering nature of existence and its characteristically cruel presentation. But, intriguingly, not in the way that held man as the victim by default.

What these philosophers forwarded so bluntly and unapologetically brought an uncomfortable focus upon all of the dirty, uncouth, and despicable tendencies of mankind. Fyodor Dostoevsky made this point clearly with statements like:

"People speak sometimes about the "bestial" cruelty of man, but that is terribly unjust and offensive to beasts, no animal could ever be so cruel as a man, so artfully, so artistically cruel."

We prefer to think of ourselves in the best light possible. Philosophy so often, in its efforts to highlight that which is good and virtuous, neglects the more base states of man. Or at least under-exemplifies the degree to which they exist in the world writ large.

The existentialists force us to look, unblinkingly, at the depths of our own depravity. There is a brash honesty that tastes bitter to the tongue while remaining self-evidently true. The sense that rationalism and rationality itself are a laughable attempt to compartmentalize the pathological sides of our own nature. That there exists an inescapable and oddly fundamental part of our being that yearns for destruction. Destruction of our world, destruction of our relationships, even destruction of ourselves.

Dostoevsky, in his cynical masterpiece — *Notes from the Underground* — gave air to the self-destructive prerogative of man in the following claim:

"Shower upon him every earthly blessing, drown him in a sea of happiness, so that nothing but bubbles of bliss can be seen on the surface; give him economic prosperity, such that he should have nothing else to do but sleep, eat cakes and busy himself with the continuation of his species, and even then out of sheer ingratitude, sheer spite, man would play you some nasty trick.

He would even risk his cakes and would deliberately desire the most fatal rubbish, the most uneconomical absurdity, simply to introduce into all this positive good sense his fatal fantastic element.

It is just his fantastic dreams, his vulgar folly that he will desire to retain, simply in order to prove to himself-as though that were so necessary - that men still are men and not the keys of a piano, which the laws of nature threaten to control SO completely that soon one will be able to desire nothing but by the calendar.

And that is not all: even if man really were nothing but a piano-key, even if this were proved to him by natural science and mathematics, even then he would not become reasonable, but would purposely do something perverse out of simple ingratitude, simply to gain his point.

And if he does not find means he will contrive destruction and chaos, will contrive sufferings of all sorts, only to gain his point!

I believe in it, I answer for it, for the whole work of man really seems to consist in nothing but proving to himself every minute that he is a man and not a piano-key!"

From the theological point of view, what he and the other existentialists describe speak to the very real and so often avoided topic of evil. What Dostoevsky explores in the nature of man, the theological defines as a nature of being. Something that is existent within total existence itself. A spirit. An element. Something base and universal.

Evil, as a concept, is as insufficient to express its being as rationality is to defineman's. Those who have come into contact with real evil, who experience its weight, speak to the sense of being that it has. That there is a presence. Some *thing* as opposed to some concept. It has been enough to make faithful believers in God simply because they have known His opposite. Theologically, it is intrinsic to man. Something that is inescapable this side of the afterlife.

We harbor a darkness as part of our very nature. Carl Jung spoke very directly, and with urgency, regarding the 'Shadow Self' or the 'Dark Passenger'. How, in the unconscious side of our being, darkness lurks as a natural counterweight to every virtuous or noble thing we strive for. He famously analogized this when he wrote:

"No tree, it is said, can grow to heaven unless its roots reach down to hell."

To say that man is intrinsically flawed is to say almost nothing at all. If our very nature tends to lean as often towards evil (whether overt or banal) as it does towards good, what hope can we truly have (as individuals or a society) that man can mitigate his own deleterious nature?

There is a story of a man who once asked a preacher, "Why would God allow so much suffering in the world? If He were good, how could he allow such wanton evil?" The priest replied, "I understand your question, but what if God were to ask you the same thing?".

How much of the evil that exists in the world is wrought by man himself? How much suffering is due, in part or in whole, to that side of our own nature that seeks destruction, even self-immolation, to consciously or unconsciously prove we are not a piano-key? And were we to discover the degree to which it was our fault, would we strive to combat it if we knew how?

In the Christian tradition, we are considered evil, corrupt beings by default since the fall of man through the original sin of Adam and Eve. Sin, and thus evil, has been presented as our birthright since mankind began. In very much the same way that Dostoevsky would make the case that a man is not a man absent his darker nature, Christianity states that every human being born into this life is considered burdened by this corruption as a matter of being.

Interestingly, Christianity's solution to the suffering effects of this inextricable dilemma are known, epistemically, to necessarily stem from outside of mankind for the very sake of this nature. The idea that man is faulty by default, begs the solution to it originate from outside of man himself.

All of this circles back towards the existence of, and truly the necessity of, a higher order moral imperative. The *ought* that is preordinate to the *is*. A real, transcendental moral Truth that we, as intrinsically corrupted beings, can strive towards as a true standard of virtue. Knowing all the while that our dark nature exists and persists, yet aiming at an impossible goal not constructed by man, yet constructed for him.

Nietzsche attempted to reconstruct this formula, apart from any transcendentality, through his construct of the Übermensch. The one critical flaw in that construct was the fact that man must determine for himself what his own highest moral standards are before he could strive towards attaining them. In light of the persistent presence of Jung's 'Shadow Self', any proprietary conception of a moral standard would inevitably present an ever shifting sliding-scale, dependent on each individual's understanding and mastery of its effects within their conscious ego. The end result of that effort can be seen in any number of theologically nascent power structures and their innate tendency to err towards eventual totalitarianism and collapse.

This is the offer of Christianity. That moral Truth exists apart from man's conception of it. That we, as a naturally destructive creature, cannot attain it. But, through the grace of something higher than our fallen selves, we may aspire towards and achieve proximate access to, not perfection in our nature but, salvation in spite of it.

DEATH AND THE ETHEREAL

Being that the theological pillar uniquely holds claim (via faith) in an extra material, ethereal layer of Truth, it is natural and, in fact, appropriate that it offers hope beyond the cessation of material life.

It has become an age-old trope and an endemic quality of those who denounce this pillar that they become more unsure of the reality of an afterlife the closer they come to finding out for themselves.

The common wartime adage is "No atheists in foxholes". If you believe (through a wholesale reliance on rationalistic materialism) that all we are is the sum of our material parts, then the death of that structure *must* be the total annihilation of our being. And yet, when that absolute end nears (as in wartime foxholes), one can be forgiven for a rethinking of this worldview in the face of its enormity.

Consider the following as a thought experiment: What if a human being was presented in front of you and then died in a way that only minimally damaged their body. If there were a way to freeze their state and repair the mortal damage that killed them, some time in the future, would they come back to life?

We can witness minor versions of this with dying people being resuscitated by CPR or defibrillator paddle shocks. But in this case, the person is fully and finally dead. What exactly is missing from that structure to bring the person back?

Put another way, if you were (through some marvel of future technology) able to recreate — atom for atom, cell for cell — the exact and total body of some long dead person from 1000 years ago, would they awaken alive?

This would seem like a straight-forward affirmative answer to an ardent materialist. But when fully considered, it runs directly back into Chalmer's "Hard" problem of consciousness. The contention that the sum of the "Easy" problems don't, in actuality, account for the conscious experiential qualia of existence.

The very fact that those in elite positions within computer advancement and AI theory think that consciousness will simply "emerge" from some unknown base threshold for it to exist within a computer, speaks to the fact that we don't know what that threshold — or more to the point, what consciousness itself — is at all. How can we, from that position of ignorance, make any sweeping proclamation that the essence of a sentient being — the soul — is and must be a mere affect of material infrastructure?

In nearly every theological tradition there exists the idea of a passing on from material existence to an ethereal one. Whether into another instantiation of mortal existence (in the case of reincarnation) or onto another layer of existence beyond and apart from that of the material. The fact that those who relegate these beliefs to mere antiquated superstition don't actually know anything more about the possibility of a transcendent ethereal layer after death. This speaks not to their wisdom but to their lack of that most precious commodity of the theological — faith.

If it were in fact the case that there are more layers to total reality than just those material ones we have the most access to, the only pillar one could expect to find anything to say about these supra-material levels would have to be the theological. I believe it's because of this fact that we find afterlife traditions in every spiritual belief system man has ever adhered to. Simply put, if there is life after death, from this side of the veil, our only avenue to parse its reality is through faith.

We, as mortals, are ill-equipped to comprehend death merely through rationalism. It needs to be understood experientially, which, of course cannot be done while alive.

Science can only speak to the material. Philosophy can only speak to what man knows. Anything beyond those considerations requires the reinforcement of faith.

This is why I do not believe we will find a reductionist answer to consciousness and why any hope to stretch ourselves towards layers of Truth beyond our physical ones must rely heavily on a theological pillar of understanding.

When you accept this as a prerequisite starting point for your considerations of death, the icy grip it holds on a materialistic worldview will melt under the dawn of hope, through faith, in what lies beyond this physical existence.

A HIGHER POWER

One of the primary issues that obscures our view of and access to the total Truth, to emmet, is stated clearly in the subtitle of this book — *Navigating the Objective from the Subjective*. We exist (as laid out in the introductory chapter) restricted by our subjective view within total Truth. Our inability to know it, or even the breadth of it, constrains our access to any knowledge of its totality.

The theological pillar makes two unique claims that set it apart from the other two. Both of which are predicated on its primary feature, that of faith. The first is that there is a total Truth that includes ethereal considerations as fundamental. And the second is that total Truth is itself an aspect of God. That you can both seek and commune with Truth, and that those before you have done so with success.

In the Hindu beliefs, it's characterized as a totalizing, phenomenological, universal consciousness — Brahman. In the Upanishads, it states:

> "In the beginning this was Self alone, [...] He looking round saw nothing but his Self."

A similar statement is found in the Gospel of John, regarding the totality of God from the beginning:

> "In the beginning was the Word, and the Word was with God, and the Word was God."

Further *apophatic* verses — Biblical writings that state a qualitative difference between God and anything else — like John 14:6, define God (in the person of Jesus) as such:

"I am the way and the truth and the life..."

These statements of faith unequivocally present God as Truth itself. As a universal, total Truth. Because if God *is* Truth and God existed from the beginning, then emmet — total Truth — is a fundamental quality of God.

If we were to take that — upon faith — as axiomatic, then man's search for Truth (that he cannot know by himself from his subjective position) is, in effect, his search for God.

God (being Truth) and Truth (being complete) embody an unattainable understanding while simultaneously presenting it as a qualitative *good* to strive towards. This presents more than simply a difference in layers; it's a difference between our proprietary understanding and everything that is in relation to everything that is.

The acceptance of this, our position in emmet as compared to emmet as a unified, conscious thing, absolutely necessitates humility. The contrast should be humbling in its very consideration. But the real reinforcing power of the theological pillar is not simply recognizing our impossible lack when compared to a universal whole; it's our ability, and truly our necessity, to plead its intersession when we come up against the struggles of our limited position.

Having and believing in a higher power both presents man with inspiration and accountability in its heights, while simultaneously offering the comfort of a Truth beyond our vision in our lows. Through faith in what we cannot see from our limited perspective, resilience springs forth in the face of impossible tasks.

What's more, holding a higher order superordinate power by default above and beyond the reach of man, makes man's corrupt attempts to usurp its authority a vain and doomed effort. This presents a break-water against overreaches of the state at the level of the individual who answers to a higher power than it. As an aggregate effect at the level of the communal, those people who hold Truth as preordinate to man build more lasting communities through their experientially based beliefs than those who answer first to the state.

This is an apt time to be reminded of the distinction that Jung made in *The Undiscovered Self*. That is, the distinction between *creeds* and *religion*. The latter is, and *must* be, representative of a personal, experiential understanding of God. While the former serves (when theology is held monolithically instead of in triune with the other two pillars) as indistinguishable from a totalitarian state. Thus it's imperative that the theological, when recognized and implemented for its vital aspects, be regarded as fundamentally appropriate and qualifiable from the layer of the individual at a consciousness, or soul, level.

CLOSING OF THE CIRCLE

In the introduction of this book, we laid out a number of concepts parsed into constructs to use as analogies. The three pillars. Layers of reality. Total Truth and its constituents between those layers.

One of the other constructs we used was that of a spectrum. One whereby we may conceptualize a continuum that moves in a linear sense from empirical science on the left, through philosophy in the middle, and into ethereal theology on the right.

There is much that can be said regarding that construct and the interaction between all three major portions along a sliding scale. Though there is another adaptation of this construct that I alluded to early on. One that adds another dimension and a revolutionary interaction to the polar opposite ends of its linear constraints.

In the final chapter of my focus on "Reality" in the book *Consciousness Reality & Purpose*, I explored an old and mystic school of thought that is, these days, referred to as Hermeticism. The most modern and most publicly recognized text within this school was an early 20th century amalgamation of their beliefs called *The Kybalion*.

In The Kybalion, focus is brought upon what are termed the seven principals of Hermeticism. Without going back through all seven (which we did in the previous book), I'd like to draw focus to one that affords this extra dimensional perception of our linear spectrum above. That is the fourth hermetic principal: *The Principal of Polarity.*

The Principal of Polarity states that everything is dual; all things have an opposite. More to the point, this apparent duality is itself a hidden whole. Hot and cold are exactly the same thing, in essence, but vary only in degree. As does quiet and loud, dark and light, large and small, etc. This idea simultaneously represents a linear spectrum and a completed circle when fully considered.

Think of a coin. It has two sides, yet they both meet at the edge. There is a connection between total opposites that make them unite as a whole. Part of the fourth hermetic principal explicitly states that extremes meet at their poles. This cannot be properly understood from the concept of a linear spectrum; those extremes only get further from each other. Picture, instead, a spectrum so long that it curves back upon itself. At the totalizing of this reciprocal curve from each pole, a uniting of opposites will create (instead of a line) a closed circle!

There exists a connection between the scientific and the theologic pillars that isn't mediated through the philosophic but is an actual communal union between total polar opposites to close the circle; in effect, binding duality (in the hermetic sense) into a harmonious whole.

Knowing that the strength of the scientific is proof and the strength of the theologic is faith, it should come as no surprise that this unification happens at the crossroads of those two features.

Science, no matter what you want to use it for, requires faith before a starting point can be proposed from which to empirically explore. These can be considered as axioms, a priori assumptions, or hypotheses.

Rupert Sheldrake, in his book *Morphic Resonance: The Nature of Formative Causation,* referenced this connection when citing famed psychonaut Terrance McKenna's observations about science:

"As Terence McKenna observed, "Modern science is based on the principle: 'Give us one free miracle and we'll explain the rest.' The one free miracle is the appearance of all the mass and energy in the universe and all the laws that govern it in a single instant from nothing."

This idea of "one free miracle" is a sardonic, yet acute, observation that all rationalism (and even empiricism) start from an axiom of faith in the unknown. Belief is a fundamental prerequisite before any work towards a scientific endeavor can commence. It's not even disputed in the sciences; quite the contrary, it is enshrined as a formative component in the scientific process!

At every step along the way, faith must be invoked before work can begin. This is the union, the completion of the ring, between the poles of the scientific and the theologic. What we look at so diametrically as a zero-sum comparison — either you believe in science or you believe in theology — is in reality a false dichotomy clouding our understanding of a glorious whole. A vital unity that gives strength and utility to every effort of man to divine his perception of the Truth.

THE RETURN OF GOD

Mankind, through his many different eras and forms, has ever wandered and struggled through the mires of a short, chaotic life. Straining to orient and rationalize an infinite landscape of pain, love, danger, and triumph. We, as individuals, are a steady-state of change. Yet we as a whole are nothing if not predictably cyclical.

The cycles of man are ancient and ever-repeating. Yet we so often look at ourselves and our lives as novel and unexpected. This difference of layers breeds a form of meta-level myopia that C.S. Lewis referred to as "chronological snobbery". The idea that we — as the most current versions of mankind — must necessarily be greater than and not subject to the faulty natures of our forebears. Though, historically, we seem to fall prey over and over to the mistakes of the past.

It is seen through the cultural cycles of empires that are so clearly laid out in books like William Strauss' *The Fourth Turning*. An idea that can be summed up with the adage:

Hard times make hard men.

Hard men bring good times.

Good times make weak men.

Weak men bring hard times.

The cycle that I see playing out in our present time seems to be a turning from the spiritual 'hard times' that a theologically deficient and weakened society has wrought upon itself after fitfully discarding one of the strengths that built the good times they were born into.

Like the mythological phoenix who dies in fire only to be reborn from its ashes, there appears to be a bursting forth of the theological in the Western world as if to say, "I am here, as I've always been.".

It may be that the reports of the death of God have been greatly exaggerated or, at least, entirely misunderstood. Like holding your breath under water doesn't mean you no longer need air, the dismantling of the West's theological Chesterton's Fence may have merely been an interlude between the cycles of man's search for himself... for God — for Truth.

CHAPTER V

CONCLUSION

"The most merciful thing in the world, I think, is the inability of the human mind to correlate all its contents. We live on a placid island of ignorance in the midst of black seas of infinity, and it was not meant that we should voyage far. The sciences, each straining in its own direction, have hitherto harmed us little; but some day the piecing together of dissociated knowledge will open up such terrifying vistas of reality, and of our frightful position therein, that we shall either go mad from the revelation or flee from the light into the peace and safety of a new dark age."

— H.P. LOVECRAFT

CONCLUSION

I began the previous chapters with an introduction heavily focused on the namesake of this book. The idea — the construct — of layers of Truth. For the most part, in the proceeding three chapters thereafter, I presented and (often) only implicitly parsed some of these layers within the more explicit conceptual constructs of the three pillars.

I realize that this left a certain onus upon the reader to read some of the constructs of layers, Truth fragments, subsets, and true things into those writings. And because of that, this conclusion will make an attempt to more explicitly highlight some of these proprietary distinctions within those three pillars.

Though I will endeavor to do so in a way that's not itemized or linear in effect. Because there are still a number of meta considerations to observe and meditate upon as we close this book. And since there has been a lot of reading between the introduction and now, the best way to start our conclusionary chapter would be a summarization of the epistemic basis of this construct.

EPISTEMOLOGY OF TRUTH

In the efforts I've made to distinguish my thoughts and arrange them into a coherent concept, I (like everyone before me) ran up against the inevitable issue of determining my starting points, terminology, and constructs that best represent them.

On the surface, that would seem like an effort to simply discover and define what is true. But what that requires, in effect, is a building of the substrate upon which the very understanding of Truth can be rationalized. It required an epistemology. That is, a theory of knowledge. What defines Truth and what differentiates it from opinion.

Though, as was covered in the introduction, what that creates by default is going to simply be another proprietary, meta-ontological structure that at best serves to organize a concept and at worst will become less effective the further it branches away from its inception point.

This is the strength and weakness to all constructs. They amount to, in actuality, a more structured version of an analogy. And it's well known in the arenas of argumentation that analogies are the weakest form of debate, because they can be assailed directly while avoiding the idea that they are attempting to present. But what more can we be expected to do from our necessarily subjective position within total reality?

I recognize that this is the case with all constructs, including my own. So what I want to make clear is that I, by no means, intend for them — layers, pillars, spectrums, etc. — to be relied upon as fundamentally correct by their distinctive structures, but rather that they be employed fort he use they provide in differentiating what we encounter within total reality as well as what can be presumed by contrast.

With that being said, I have found the construct of Layers of Truth to be incredibly helpful and insightful when observing information and phenomena. With a heuristic of layering, it becomes very apparent where inappropriate or conflated conclusions are made regardless of the subject.

I can witness something that seems incoherent, recognize from where the conclusion came and compare it to where I'm considering its coherence in contrast. Is there a difference between my position and theirs? Is that because of incorrect information or a differing of layers from whence it sprung? Are they correct and I incorrect? Vice versa? Are we both correct but at different layers?

Asking these questions begins to broaden one's considerations while humbling one's presumptions. At the same time it allows a particular discernment to become evident, which allows for wisdom to be accessible with its use.

The ability to recognize distinct layers of Truth and discern appropriate relevance to your situation or position has proven invaluable in conceptualizing Truth as well as for distinguishing malicious deceptions. As was mentioned in the introduction, there are bad actors who understand how to manipulate people through conditionally true statements to cause you to act beyond those conditions in effect. Being able to view something as true from the correct layer that it is true in will prevent you from being caused to presume it true among layers that it is not.

JUST THE FACTS

There exists an idea in our culture that Truth can be discerned through the discovery of the facts. Facts are proven empirically in laboratories, courtrooms, and universities around the world. The emphasis we put on them is meant as a period at the end of a sentence. 'These are the facts — the indisputable facts!'.

Facts are gathered, guarded, and lorded over by people who presume the discovery and invocation of them grants their barer entry into the hallowed halls of Truth. It may dishearten such people, if they haven't figured it out before now, to learn that the power and eminence of a fact are closer to an illusion than the actual Truth.

The definition of a fact is essentially something that is explicitly correct. Information that is objectively true. This definition is valuable, but not as valuable as people, who revere facts, act as though it is.

I had previously alluded to the concern of bad actors who manipulate people through conditionally true statements. A fact itself is, fundamentally, only conditionally true. Allow me to demonstrate what I mean.

You may say that it's a *fact* that I am writing the words that I'm writing while I'm writing them. This would be true, but only within the very narrow parameters that are both implicitly as well as explicitly set into that statement. The fact of my writing what I'm writing is explicitly cordoned chronologically by the condition of "while I'm writing". That's one parameter. It is further implicitly assumed that what is meant by "I" is contained to the layer of my entire person. For example, my fingers are typing these words while my toes are not. It wouldn't make implicit sense to say that my toes are not me or that my fingers *are* what I am. So this implies another constraining layer that maintains the veracity of that fact to myself as a whole.

It may at first seem semantic to make those distinctions, but consider the idea of facts from within the construct of layers that was laid out in the introduction. Facts would beak into 'a true thing' in that construct. Something that is true, hierarchically, holds the lowest value point in the order of total Truth. True things — facts — are discovered then bundled together with other true things to make a coherent subset that resides within a Truth fragment that should be contained within a layer of the total Truth.

Another analogous way of thinking about them would be like the letters of the alphabet. A fact is like a singular letter. No singular letter (discounting 'I' and 'a') constitutes an entire word. Single letters are bundled together into coherent words (subsets) that serve the constricted purpose of containing meaning or intention. Words are then further coordinated into sentences, paragraphs, and completed works that (though they rely upon letters from the bottom up) represent a personalized effort to transmit thought from one person to another.

A fact is not an inherent Truth in the same way that a letter isn't an inherent thought. And this isn't to take away from its function. It's the very feature of a fact's conditionality that gives it value the same way that a letter's utility is due to each one's unique function within word creation. But it's the misunderstanding of the value and the hierarchical position of facts by people that allows for either accidental conflation or worse, intentional and malicious manipulation to take place.

In very much the same way that statistics can and do get used to correctly present misleading conclusions, the reliance and misuse of facts in proprietary narrative creation must be discretely understood if one hopes to wield the philosophical sword of discernment for themselves.

People will tell you they know the facts and then, in the same breath, require your submission to the concussion they've crafted with them. I would implore the reader to ask of themselves if the layer of the conclusion someone presents to you corresponds with the facts that lead them there.

Think of the ontological structure that is being presumed by a person proclaiming the Truth. What layers are they speaking from? What layers are they speaking to? What layers are they ignoring? By identifying these concepts within a thought or a narrative, you'll find yourself much more apt to observe any conflation of layers that so often happens during efforts to guide an outcome.

Remember we, as humans, are story tellers. It's how we understand our reality. It's not wrong in any way to absorb or create stories that are meant to be limited or allegorical. But by recognizing that this is the position we all hold as subjective viewers within the enormity of emmet, the very idea of holding one view or another can be done so with an appropriate deference. Knowing all along that no individual person can hold claim to the total Truth.

THE MECHANISTIC & PHENOMENOLOGICAL

If it's understood at this point that explicit facts don't (and can't) represent any more than a small and constrained portion of emmet, what are we to do with them? The wrong conclusion to make would be to distrust them based on their conditionality. Should they be appropriately vetted? Yes, but once reliable they need to be set to work to hold any actionable value for us. The use of facts — true things — is for them to serve a functional purpose through their varied applications. Exactly in the manner that letters do to build words.

So, in that same precept, facts are valuable to discover and understand only so far as they serve a beneficial function to those who recognize them. Consider it the difference between pouring a bucket of plastic letters in front of a two year-old or ordering those same 26 letters of the alphabet onto a computer keyboard for an adult who understands how to use them. The toddler may play with them and build towers or patterns that serve no lasting purpose while, the adult can craft transmissible knowledge and thought through a recognizable, functional lexicon that those letters are meant to build.

Were we to carry this analogy onto the next hierarchical structure in our construct, the words that letters build — that serve a utilitarian function — are akin to the subsets that people build with individual facts for the benefit they provide. You can think of subsets like words or, more accurately, like instructions. Certain bundles of facts can, and do, create mechanisms of affect. If you were to have in front of you every single fact that makes a computer work, you wouldn't be able to make a computer until you understood the proper mechanistic utility of each in sequence, in unison,

CONCLUSION | 221

and in degree. Just as knowing every ingredient in a recipe doesn't mean you know how to make the dish it's intended to produce. The appropriate use of each ingredient for their individual function is just as important as the degree of use that they're used in harmony with every other ingredient.

Perhaps now it's more apparent how important, and yet how fragile, subsets of true things are. These bundles of facts are only bundled together if they make certain machines (or words). And those machines (or subsets) only work if they're built correctly, as defined by the prescribed effect they're meant to produce.

What this presents to us, as the architects of these subsets, is a functionally infinite vista of possibility! Not just in the use of facts and subsets that we have discovered already, but how they can be added together with those of the past, present, and future between different ideas and throughout a variety of layers.

What's more, as new facts are discovered, total revolutions (like the kind described by Thomas Kuhn) are revealed to us through their addition and the contrast they provide apposed to our current conventions. In this way, subsets are also (like true things) conditionally true while objectively functional. The condition of their true-ness is defined by the successful production of an intended affect through their use. It is true that electricity makes a computer work, but nothing about electricity necessitates a computer.

Subsets, therefore, are broadly the creative endeavor of engineers. Those people who propose to create some sort of benefit in the real world through the conjunction of known facts into functional subsets — or machines. It would then seem almost strictly derivative to believe that we, as humans, use our magnificent ability to architect function out of fact in a way that is entirely mechanistic. That is to say, the discovery and implementation of effective subsets comes from our understanding of the relevant facts they consist of.

This, in the philosophy of science, is called a mechanistic approach. It's a methodology of understanding effect before producing result. And though there is much that can be said for this style of engineering functional subsets, there is another form of discovery that speaks more to the limits of what we know than the extent of the same. This kind of discovery is called the phenomenological approach.

Exploring and revealing functional subsets phenomenologically seeks to observe effects that are a result of some sort of phenomenon. Think of it like witnessing an event, let's say a volcanic eruption, and determining the effect that explosive pressures cause as opposed to engineering a better explosive where creating explosive pressures is already mechanistically understood. It's the idea that we see an effect and try to retroactively determine what caused it instead of rationalizing an effect before we then build a machine to produce it.

What's most interesting about this philosophy of creating subsets is that anything that is, by definition, a phenomenon must come from the unknown — not the known. Phenomena are emergent by nature. They surprise us. We then try to understand, recreate, and utilize their effects for our benefits.

Those effects that we were unaware of before our observation of them.

One example of this form of engineering methodology can be seen in our phenomenological observation of a bumblebee's flight. With all of the mechanistic understanding we had about what causes flight — lift, drag, velocity, air density, weight, etc. — science was perplexed that a bumblebee was even able to fly! At first, it seemed physically impossible. The weight of the bee was too large for the size of their comparably small wings. Nonetheless, fly it did. In defiance of our perception of its possibility.

We observed what presented itself as an unexpected and contradictory phenomenon. Later, upon further exploration, scientists discovered (by means of slow motion videography) that bumblebees' wings don't flap up and down like so many other animals' and insects' wings do; instead they move in almost a figure-eight motion that creates a vortex of wind to cause the necessary lift their body size requires. This knowledge was discovered through the phenomenology of observing a demonstrable effect before understanding why it was happening.

The powerful difference between these two methods of subset creation and discovery is the meta level realization that all subsets are conditionally true and relationally relevant to our understanding of facts and their use cases. What can further be gleaned from that consideration is the degree to which our *ignorance* of what is possible is based on simply how much we don't know.

Or how much we *don't know* that we don't know!

We routinely discover entire layers of Truth that, as far as humanity was concerned prior to then, didn't exist. That means that, rationally speaking, the degree to which we don't know what we don't know is functionally infinite! And our creation, discovery, and application of proprietary subsets, in that case, are themselves just as infinite!

I cannot help but come to a place of humility and awe when considering the above. It should give inspiration to those curious observers in the sciences while at the same time chastising those who hold themselves aloft upon what amounts to an infinitesimally small portion of total Truth.

LAYERS OF TRUTH

Finally, as we move up as far as we can through the hierarchy of this construct of total Truth, we reach 'layers'.

In the introduction, we made another (somewhat) semantic sub-category within layers called Truth fragments. I want to take the time to vividly explain and illuminate what I mean with both of these concepts so that I may go further than them, into the meta of their utility.

It's my hope that you can use the five-step construct validation method in the introduction chapter, when need be, to help define varying layers in their distinctiveness. But, in all honesty, I find their distinctions most often to be self-evident to an honest observer.

Since we exist so encumbered in the material layers of reality, I'll use a few of those different layers to make the point in a way that every person should be able to understand, regardless of any specific knowledge.

Were we to look at a human and their material experience, you could witness a distinction between their physical body and the conscious mind that pilots it. This was a distinction that the philosophical theologies, like those of the Hindus and the Buddhists, illuminated in detail thousands of years ago. It was one that came into more modern philosophical vogue through the idea of Cartesian dualism in the works of René Descartes where a critical distinction was set between the mind and body of a person. Thus presenting their duality.

If we were to take these examples, I would suggest that the mind and the body of the same person are two different layers of Truth.

There are countless autonomic functions of the body that the mind is not responsible for. Everything from cellular functions to blinking and breathing. Those facts would be, realistically, categorized into the layer of the human body.

There are a cornucopia of different functions of the human mind — like emotion, rationality, individuality, as well as other conscious and unconscious qualia — that would be, most appropriately, categorized into the layer of the human mind.

Between these two layers of the same whole, interplay occurs and is necessary for a harmonious union of dualistic existence. But a conflation of these two, for any of a number of reasons (psychological, social, cultural), will lead to an inevitably destructive failure of whatever subset tried to force a fact into the wrong layer.

I witness this most often when people try to effect change through the physical to attempt to amend an issue in the cognitive or spiritual. This can be seen through the first world's reliance on pharmaceuticals to repair mental or emotional distress. They're trying to effect change in the mind through the layer of the body. And though there is an interplay between those two layers, to conflate them as the same thing completely misses the root within the mind. It's like watering your neighbor's grass waiting for your own to green from it.

There are people who, in their minds, believe they're in the wrong bodies. All sorts of ill-fated attempts can be made to bend their bodies into the impossible shape their minds want. The problem is that they're addressing the wrong layer. They're not the same thing. Regardless of the interconnection or reliance those layers have upon a healthy union.

It's the interconnection, I believe, that is the culprit for so many of the conflationary mistakes we make that wind up building doomed subsets. Machines that cannot work for their intended function in any sort of natural or long-term manner. Without the ability to recognize and understand differing layers of Truth, we can trip over our own feet in the presumption that all facts exist afloat in a singular whole that can be glued together into any proprietary ontology without objective ramifications.

It's, in fact, the fractal version of this concept where I believe the idea of Truth fragments is useful as an aid. If you conceptualize the total Truth into layers, then you can appropriately explore *within* the totality of each individual layer. Witnessing its boundaries and discovering its relationships with other tangential layers it connects to. All the while without making the mistake of mis-categorizing a true thing into a layer it doesn't belong.

In this way you can become an expert within a layer, expanding the breadth of the fragment of that layer you understand while respecting its limitations. This can act as a benefit, to those doing the exploration, that should prevent the presumption that any layer they explore *is* the total Truth, to the derision (or attempted negation) of all other layers.

Remember, it's each individual's responsibility to curate their personal ontologies — the facts and subsets that represent all they know. This process perpetually redefines the subjective reality that we each perceive around us. We — all of us — exist in a virtual reality that *is not real*. It is the culmination of what we've discovered and accepted as true that projects an emergent facsimile — an illusion of — what is the Truth.

Our ability to further and further resolve our aggregated knowledge base of emmet, though helpful in its utility, is always bound to be finite and unrepresentative of the total Truth. The perpetual discovery of brand new layers of Truth —whether psychological, material, or ethereal—is a reminder of our finite state of perception from within them.

A question then arises once you on-board the construct of layers. How do they connect as a whole? Do they stack, like a two-dimensional tower?

Do they diverge side to side based upon their differences, presenting more of a staggered or zig-zag ascension? What is the connection, and what are their properties? These are the meta considerations I'd like to present in this conclusion.

Let's go back to a distinction that was made in our look at Truth in theology. I made an important distinction between a complicated system and a complex system. The important difference between the two has to do with a holistic unification between variables in the case of a complex system, while a complicated system presents itself as more linear or derivative in its totality.

If you were to take the analogy of a Jenga tower, that would be a good representative of a complicated system. Where, although there is a systematic construction to it, any affect projected onto the tower could have an accurately estimated (or even calculated) result.

A complex system, in comparison, is defined not only in its raw complexity but in a multi-faceted harmony of interconnectivity that is bound to emit emergent results from any affects cast into any part of its whole. A good corollary for our purposes would be the neural net within a human brain. From the level of individual neurons and synapses up, what the totality of its complex system equates to is a virtual *galaxy* of nodes. And the interconnection between them all is such that any changes, additions, deletions, or even the proprietary sequences of all of them, produce unexpected results.

To extrapolate on that analogy, in chapter 12 of my previous book (a chapter titled *Cognitive Reality*) I cited scientist and researcher Brian Roemmele who made the comparison of human memory to that of a hologram. With a holographic projection, what produces a three-dimensional image in space is the intersection of many different lights. Where each beam intersects could be thought of as akin to a pixel in the total image. The more densely you pack them together or the further you space them apart will add shape and contrast between the pixels of light and the voids that separate them. This particular analogy was used by Roemmele when discussing how when scientists attempted to locate and delete a memory in a human brain, they were never quite able to do so. They may be able to somewhat obscure or corrupt the memory in part, but they could never fully delete it. It was determined through these efforts that memories aren't stored as though they were just some complicated archive; they are cast, in a decentralized manner, across the complex galaxy of neural nodes within the brain! It was the unique union and intersection of all of these disparate nodes within our cognitive complex that projected memories to us as if they were holographic in design.

It's from this kind of consideration that I would like to propose an extra-dimensional construct regarding the connections of layers within total Truth. It could be that — unlike any linear or tangential tower of layering — what the totality of emmet acts like is more representative of a complex neural net of layers.

From where we stand, primarily in the physical layers of reality, there are entirely unexpected and novel layers of reality being discovered all the time. Think of the world before we discovered the cell, the quantum, dark matter, epigenetics, or any other field we didn't know that we didn't know about — before we did. In the words of H.P. Lovecraft that we began this chapter with, they would have been discovered from our venturing out into the "black seas of infinity" beyond our "placid islands of ignorance". In theory, if we're discovering entire facets — or layers — of reality that simply did not exist within our total conception of reality before, then the possible amount of layers we don't know that we don't know can be considered functionally infinite. In Dr. Jordan Peterson's framework, everything we don't know is akin to chaos. And the quality of chaos is a state of unknowing. If we cannot expect the unexpected, then there is no theoretical limit to it.

The concept of total Truth is, like all hypotheses, predicated on a presumption. And presumption is that part of exploration that relies upon faith. Like the winding of our spectrum of pillars into a ring that connects at its extremes, I proposed the a priori presumption that there *is* a total Truth. That, if there is a totality of all things and there is something true about them all, there must be a total Truth.

It's between the consideration of all of these thoughts above that I view our efforts to know the totality of Truth as unavoidably flawed. As a hologram projects perceivable images through what *is* (points of light) and what is *missing* (voids of light), we by dint of our inevitably lacking knowledge base — whether through the constraints of what we know or the infinity of what we don't — will forever be relegated to some form of illusion of Truth.

That's not to say that Truth—emmet—doesn't exist. But that our attempts to discover its entirety are hopeless at best and vanity at worst. This acceptance should forever humble our hubris. It should rebuke each of our individual perceptions of reality enough to breed empathy and humility between those of differing views.

In the venturing of the sciences, the philosophical piecing together of dissociated knowledge, and the theological act of opening up terrifying vistas that illuminate our frightful position therein, what are we to do? Lovecraft would suggest we either go mad from the revelation or flee from the light into the peace and safety of a new dark age. And this has been a trend in human history throughout the centuries and the civilizations that embodied them. We claw, we fight, and we plant our flags upon some limited ontological reality, then demand others to accept it as whole. All the while missing the point of our meager position from which we must reside.

The point of this exploration into Truth, and even the construct I built to try and parse it with, couldn't possibly, *ever* be to *know* emmet as a whole. My hope is that it serves as a useful outline or heuristic — a guide for those who desire a balancing of whatever perception of reality they will have to inevitably build. That their worldview be a communal harmony between the pillars and throughout all the layers of Truth that they continually find along the way.

EPILOGUE

A PERSONAL NOTE FROM THE AUTHOR

In much the same way that the writing of my first book, *Consciousness Reality & Purpose* stemmed from an unexpected culmination of thoughts that aggregated over hundreds of podcasting episodes, this book was birthed and grew in a similarly unexpected way.

I, as an observer and public commentator on current affairs and their societal impacts, found it perpetually confounding how differing peoples, organizations, or politics could look at (ostensibly) the same thing and come to ardent, polar opposite conclusions.

Was it just that one side was always lying while the other always told the Truth? Such a one-dimensional take seemed absurd to consider. Although, from within any given group's perception of reality, it seemed like that was exactly the case!

I needed to dig into what exactly was going on that presented such varied and diametrically opposed worldviews. Partly because I knew it couldn't be as simple as one person and their adherents got it all right. And partly because the widening difference between groups who opposed each others fundamentality was leading towards real, global, social disorder.

Of the many different people I had the opportunity to speak with over the pandemic years of 2021 through 2023 — friends, family, teachers, doctors, scientists, philosophers, politicians, journalists —I began to track the nuances of Truth from a variety of angles. And in doing do, I unexpectedly began an internal journey that came with it.

If every individual's proprietary, ontological perspective of reality was only a limited (and often externally curated) version of the actual objective Truth, well... *I'm* part of everybody too!

Much of what I talk about in Layers of Truth, although meant as an impersonal perspective, was very much informed by my own personal introspection. Anything that sounds like an indictment upon any aspect of science, philosophy, or theology came firstly from my own personal admission of shortcomings I came to recognize in myself.

When I stated that I believe people require work within all three vital pillars for the sake of a well-balanced worldview, that's not because I presumed that I was at the end state of that endeavor myself. Quite the opposite. Throughout my own life I have run afoul of many of the pitfalls of over-relying on only one or two of those pillars at a time.

I grew up in a middle-income Christian household in Western Canada through the decades of the 1980s and 90s. From the time that I was a child until my early thirties, I relied heavily on a Christian worldview supplemented by any science I could find that corroborated it. But by the age of 32, I found myself led away from the faith of my youth by persuasive philosophically minded scientific atheists like Sam Harris. Recognizing many of the same faults that Nietzsche did in the Christian orthodoxy and reinforced by the modern determinism of the New Atheists like Harris, I abandoned my primary pillar to fallow while I built up the philosophic and scientific to take its place.

The following years, that made up the majority of my thirties, were an effort in self-discovery apart from the theological roots that so informed my formative years. Yet, in much the same way that Friedrich Nietzsche and C.S. Lewis had before me, my obfuscation and derision of the spiritual led to a vacuum where nihilism grew. I found myself, through a mixture of dissatisfaction with a job I was stuck in and the lack of any hope beyond my own power to change it, becoming quite significantly depressed. I had no hope beyond meager efforts to surf an ever-darkening sea of chaos. As just another doomed creature on a meaningless planet, nothing of the logic or rationalism that girded that perspective was of any help to me.

It took the global pandemonium of the SARS-CoV-2 pandemic to cause me to rethink my uniform reliance on the sciences and of man's morality when pressed to the fire. I watched as the rot of Moloch in the academic, medical, and political arenas took hold of my society, my friends, and my family alike. False narratives, confusing contradictions, and diametric perspectives became the daily diet for the hearts and minds of everyone around me — myself included.

Due to the lack of a uniformly stabilizing triumvirate between the Truth in science, the Truth in philosophy, and the Truth in theology, the majority of humanity became swept up in a global madness. Belgian professor of clinical psychology, Mattias Desmet, came to popularity when he defined this maddening affect within a confused and vulnerable population as "mass formation" (sometimes called mass formation psychosis). The functional mechanism of which stems from an appeal to group think through a uniform stressor, met by a rallying force to relieve it. The biggest problem with this state of mass formation is that anyone who doesn't adhere to the narrative of the mass becomes its default opposition.

My family and I found ourselves on the receiving end of the Canadian version of this phenomenon when we refused a culturally required, novel medical intervention that was necessary to be in the mass. One that, by the power of science and of the first world's monolithic trust in it, held no space for any consideration that didn't end with its prescribed and carefully curated version of reality.

It was in part due to the pressures of what would amount to years of societal ostracization that I would find myself being *again* diverted from my overreliance, *this time*, in a scientific and philosophically steeped worldview. This diversion brought me circuitously back towards faith and towards God. The pillar that I, by my own folly, left to atrophy nearly a decade before.

It was also in part due to the process of writing this book that I —through my own honest introspection —realized how withered the theological pillar was within my personal, subjective ontology of reality. I found myself convicted by my own writings when I held my current worldview up to their ideal. This, like the very inception of this book, became an unexpected blessing to me.

When I was getting close to completing the Truth in Theology chapter, I had the pleasure of several long, in-depth talks with a friend, Graham Wardle. Graham is an actor, an artist, and a deeply contemplative spiritual thinker. In one of these conversations, where I was explaining the writing and premise of this book to him, he asked me a question. One that was something I hadn't cognizantly considered before but was (as it would turn out) a deep subconscious driver behind this entire project. He asked me "If there was one thing that you wanted for your readers to get from reading this book, what would it be?".

I had never even considered that before he asked it, and yet the answer was immediately apparent to me. More than anything, I hoped that those who read this book would be able to see the value of the humility that becomes self-evident when you see how limited our perceptions are. How, in comparison to emmet, we can *never* lay claim to absolute Truth.

Through the applications of constructs like layers and pillars, my hope was that we may avoid the pitfalls of man's hubris while at the same time being able to clearly recognize them in those who would manipulate us by our limited understanding — as if *they* know the *actual* Truth.

Most of all, I would hope that in a world subsumed by nihilistic material reductionism lauded by a mololithically scientific worldview, that they — like me — could find the hope and faith that they're missing.

~ Drew Weatherhead

www.ingramcontent.com/pod-product-compliance
Lightning Source LLC
Chambersburg PA
CBHW031931160426
43209CB0003 7B/1965/J